D1536083

Walt Disney's
WORLD OF THE
DRAGONLORDS

by Byron Erickson and Giorgio Cavazzano

featuring

Huey, Dewey & Louie, Donald Duck, and Uncle Scrooge

GEMSTONE PUBLISHING
Timonium Maryland

Stephen A. Geppi
President/Publisher and Chief Executive Officer

John K. Snyder Jr.
Chief Administrative Officer

STAFF
Leonard (John) Clark
Editor-in-Chief

Sue Kolberg
Assistant Editor

Travis Seitler
Art Director

David Gerstein
Archival Editor

Melissa Bowersox
Director - Creative Projects

CONTRIBUTING STAFF
Gary Leach
Susan Daigle-Leach
Art & Editorial

ADVERTISING/ MARKETING
J.C. Vaughn
Executive Editor

Arnold T. Blumberg
Editor

Brenda Busick
Creative Director

Jamie David
Director of Marketing

Sara Ortt
Marketing Assistant
ads@gemstonepub.com

Heather Winter
Office Manager
Toll Free
(888) 375-9800
Ext. 249

Mark Huesman
Production Assistant

Mike Wilbur
Shipping Manager

Mike Kacala
Inventory Coordinator

www.gemstonepub.com

WORLD OF THE DRAGONLORDS

Story by Byron Erickson
Art by Giorgio Cavazzano
Lettering & Titles by Jon Babcock
Color by Susan Daigle-Leach, Barry Grossman,
　　　　Marie Javins, Scott Rockwell
Cover Art by Giorgio Cavazzano
Layout by Sue Kolberg

TABLE OF CONTENTS

Walt Disney's *World of the Dragonlords* Published by Gemstone Publishing, 1966 Greenspring Drive, Timonium MD.
© 2005 Disney Enterprises, Inc. except where noted. All rights reserved. Nothing contained herein may be reproduced in any form without the written permission of Disney Enterprises, Inc., Burbank, CA. All rights reserved. PRINTED IN CANADA

FOREWORD

by Byron Erickson

As with so many things Disney, *World of the Dragonlords* all started with a mouse. Or more accurately, a "Maus," as in *Micky Maus,* the German Disney weekly equivalent of *Walt Disney's Comics and Stories.* The market for Disney comics was going through a bad period in Germany in the late 1990s, and sales had dropped far enough that the German editors were desperate to turn things around. It was at one of many "crises" meetings in Stuttgart in early 1999 that *Dragonlords* was born, when a single image of the nephews riding around on flying dragons popped into my mind.

In hindsight I'm sure that image came to mind as a result of what the Germans were willing to try—a long story told in serial form (they wanted something that would hook the readers into coming back issue after issue). They preferred that it star Huey, Dewey, and Louie (their market research indicated that their readers identified most with Donald's nephews), and that it be a fantasy adventure, which would attract more interest than a mundane treasure hunt. And oh, yeah—it would be nice if I could get a "star" artist to draw it.

The details came later. Working off that single inspirational image, I spent the next couple of months outlining a plot, characters, and a fantasy world complex enough to justify all the pages I'd been handed, but also a story *visual* enough to tell in comics form. I also worked hard to make sure that I still had a *Disney* story, one that was grounded in Duckburg and the Ducks' personalities, one that moved and was motivated by who they are and how they relate to one another.

At some point in the plotting process, I realized that what I had here was a story about the Duck *family:* thrown into and separated by a war, but always struggling to come together again. This family theme is mirrored by other characters—most specifically the baby dragons and their mother—and maybe something is learned about families along the way, or maybe it's something we all already know but sometimes forget to remember. What that is I'll leave to the readers to figure out for themselves.

I still needed a "star artist" to draw the story, and I always had only one man in mind for *Dragonlords*—Giorgio Cavazzano, star artist among star artists and Italian pocketbook artist supreme. Giorgio and I had collaborated before in 1997 on "Secret of the Incas" (*Uncle Scrooge Adventures* 53-54), a long story we did to celebrate Uncle Scrooge's 50th birthday. Since Giorgio generally works as a freelance artist for Disney Italy, all contact between us was filtered through them. Although ultimately successful, the experience was frustrating for both of us because we couldn't communicate directly.

This frustration was finally addressed in June 1999 when I traveled to Cavazzano's home in Merano, Italy (near Venice) to pitch the *Dragonlords* plot to him. During the course of my pitch, Giorgio added a number of improvements and enhancements to the story, and a lot

3

of good gag ideas, and the visit ended with him agreeing to draw the entire series—with the proviso that we worked directly, a condition I was only too willing to accept. It should be mentioned here that because I don't speak Italian, "directly" meant using the translation skills of Teresa Zemolin, the wife of Alessandro Zemolin, Cavazzano's long-time inker. I'll be forever grateful for her help and assistance (and guilty that she had to translate so many pages of such long-winded manuscripts).

Shortly after our meeting, Giorgio drew up a series of character sketches that completely influenced the course of the series. They were so "spot on" that every time I needed help getting back into a character's personality, I had only to look at those sketches to remember whom I was writing about. And as the chapters rolled along, I only had to look at Giorgio's marvelous finished artwork to inspire me anew to do a third or even a fourth rewrite; I was determined that my scripts would be worthy of his talents. As you can tell, I'm certainly happy with what Giorgio has drawn—his artwork is so much more than lively, stunning, and emotional, but it would take ten more pages to describe how and why. Your time would be better spent just looking at the pictures.

Dragonlords took a little over two years to write and draw, and by the time it was finished, the situation in Germany had changed. Sales were back up (the comics business has always been cyclical), editors had changed, and the people in charge were no longer willing to publish such a "radical" series in the *Micky Maus* weekly. To be fair, no publisher in the Nordic countries was willing, either (12 chapters and 164 pages seems to be the deal killer here). The story languished in a file drawer until 2003, when the Germans finally began to serialize *Dragonlords* in

Donald Duck Sonderheft, a monthly comic aimed at fans and collectors. Shortly thereafter, Italy followed suit with publication in *Zio Paperone,* again a monthly aimed at older fans.

Ah, but then those wonderful people at Sanoma in Finland collected all 12 chapters into a book, complete with a brand-new cover by Giorgio Cavazzano drawn especially for the Finnish edition. And they even put my name on the cover! Seriously, this edition was a dream come true. Despite the fact that I consciously wrote a story I knew would be serialized, I'd hoped even from the beginning that someday it would be published complete in one book. "If only," I thought, "I could convince Sanoma to publish an English edition just for me…" Now, of course, several years later Gemstone has done exactly that.

So thanks to John, Sue, David, Travis, and everyone else at Gemstone for their faith in the story, and especially thanks to you, the discerning American readers, for buying the book.

WORLD OF THE DRAGONLORDS
CHAPTER 1:
A DOOR OPENS... AND CLOSES!

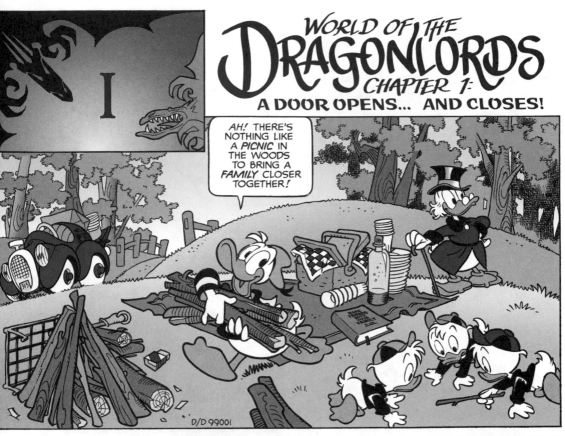

AH! THERE'S NOTHING LIKE A *PICNIC* IN THE WOODS TO BRING A *FAMILY* CLOSER TOGETHER!

D/D 99001

OR AS DOC SCHMOCK SO *WISELY* WRITES, "THE FAMILY THAT *PICNICS* TOGETHER, *BONDS* TOGETHER!"

GOSH, I CAN'T WAIT UNTIL THE *HIGHLIGHT* OF THE GOOD DOCTOR'S TOGETHERNESS PICNIC PROGRAM— THE "BONDING BONFIRE"!

MAKE FRIENDS WITH YOUR FAMILY BY DOC SCHMOCK

WE'LL ALL HOLD HANDS WHILE WE *DANCE* AROUND THE BONFIRE AND SING THE "BONDING SONG"! THE BOYS WILL *LOVE* IT!

OKAY, WE'RE AGREED! WE'LL MAKE OUR *BREAK* AS SOON AS UNCA DONALD IS BUSY LIGHTING THAT *STUPID* BONFIRE!

WE'LL *SCATTER*, MEET UP AT THE TRUCK STOP ON ROUTE 101, AND *HITCH A RIDE* BACK TO *DUCKBURG*!

WE'LL HAVE TO HOPE FOR A *FAST* TRUCK! WE'VE JUST *GOT* TO GET TO RAMBLIN' STUDIOS BY 3:00!

≠GULP!≠ IF WE'RE *LATE,* WE'LL *MISS OUT* ON OUR CHANCE TO BE CAST AS *EXTRAS* IN *GALACTIC DOOM!*

DON'T EVEN *THINK* ABOUT IT! WE *WON* THAT CHANCE FAIR AND SQUARE!

GALACTIC DOOM WILL BE THE *BIGGEST* SCIENCE FICTION FILM SINCE *STAR WRECK,* AND *WE'RE* GOING TO BE *IN* IT!

THINK INSTEAD ABOUT THE *COOL COSTUMES* WE'LL GET TO WEAR!

AND ABOUT ALL THE BIG *FILM STARS* WE'LL GET TO MEET!

YEAH!

REMEMBER, THE ONLY THING STANDING IN THE WAY OF OUR DREAM COMING TRUE IS THIS *INSANE* "FAMILY TOGETHER-NESS" PICNIC!

SOME FAMILY! EVEN WHEN WE'RE *TOGETHER,* WE'RE *APART!*

UNCA DONALD IS SO CAUGHT UP IN HIS LATEST *POP PSYCH* CRAZE THAT HE DOESN'T EVEN *REALIZE* THAT FAMILIES ARE MADE UP OF *INDIVIDUALS!*

AND UNCA SCROOGE IS EVEN *WORSE!* HE ONLY CAME ALONG SO HE COULD ESTIMATE HOW MUCH *MONEY* HE CAN MAKE...

$300!

$500!

...IF HE *CLEAR CUTS* THIS SECTION OF THE BLACK FOREST!

$1000!

AND THEN THERE'S *US*—THREE VERY *SELFISH* BOYS WHO ARE PLANNING TO GO *A.W.O.L.* OVER A SCIENCE FICTION FILM!

≠GULP!≠ SOME-ONE COULD GET THE IDEA THAT THE MEMBERS OF OUR FAMILY DON'T *CARE* ABOUT THE OTHERS *AT ALL!*

I CARE, BOYS! AND YOU'LL KNOW HOW *MUCH* I CARE WHEN YOU SINK YOUR BEAKS INTO MY YUMMY *"TOGETHER-NESS"* SANDWICHES!

THEY'RE *PEANUT BUTTER* AND *PICKLED HERRING!* Dr. SCHMOCK SAYS THEY'LL REMIND US THAT OUR *LITTLE DIFFERENCES* AREN'T *IMPORTANT!*

=OOG!=

TIME TO *JOIN* THE REST OF YOUR *FAMILY,* UNCLE SCROOGE!

BUT... BUT... I HAVEN'T FINISHED MY *INVENTORY* OF THE TREES!

AH! CAN'T YOU JUST *FEEL* THE WAVES OF *TOGETHERNESS* GENTLY WASHING OVER US?!

THE ONLY THING I CAN FEEL IS *NAUSEA!*

YOUR SAND-WICHES ARE *INEDIBLE...*

READING THAT BOOK HAS OBVIOUSLY *ROTTED* YOUR ALREADY WEAK *MIND!!!*

...AND THIS *"TO-GETHER-NESS COLA"* TASTES LIKE *SEWER SLUDGE!!*

BUT... BUT...

BUT... BUT...

=ARRRR...=

=AAAARRRGHH!!!=

7

HEY, I NEVER SAID HOW *BIG* IT WOULD BE, BRENDON! I WASN'T EVEN SURE THE *SPELL* WOULD *WORK!*

BUT WHERE *ARE* WE? THIS DOESN'T LOOK LIKE *FREEDOM MARSH* TO ME!

Oh, IT'S PROBABLY *NOT!* THE ONLY THING I COULD *THINK* ABOUT WAS NOT BEING *ROASTED* IN THAT FOREST FIRE THE MORG SET!

UNDERSTAND-ABLE, OLD FRIEND! STILL, I'D LIKE TO KNOW HOW *FAR AWAY* FROM HOME WE ARE!

I GUESS WE COULD AL-WAYS *ASK* THOSE *NATIVES* OVER THERE!

BY OUR MOTHER! THEY LOOK LIKE *DUCKS!* BUT THEY'RE WEARING *CLOTHES!*

YOU THERE!

Uh-OH! I THINK IT'S TIME WE CALL OFF THIS PICNIC ON ACCOUNT OF *WEIRDOES!*

WAIT!

≈GACK!≈ REALLY *FAST* WEIRDOES!

RELAX! I'M NOT GOING TO *HURT* YOU! I JUST WANT TO KNOW *WHERE* WE ARE!

YOU... YOU MEAN WHICH *≈GULP!≈* PLANET? IT... IT'S CALLED *EARTH!*

DO YOU REALIZE WHAT THIS *MEANS,* BRENDON?! MY DOORWAY WORKED BEYOND EVEN MY *WILDEST* FANTASIES!

WHEN WE STEPPED THROUGH IT, WE STEPPED INTO *ANOTHER WORLD!*

9

OR MORE LIKELY, INTO ANOTHER *DIMENSION!* WOW! NO OTHER MAGICIAN HAS *EVER* CONJURED UP SUCH A *POWERFUL* DOORWAY!

"WAR"?

MY CONGRATULATIONS, HINTERMANN! BUT CAN WE GO THROUGH IT *AGAIN...* GET BACK TO OUR MOTHER AND THE *WAR?*

YOU'RE ALWAYS SUCH A *KILLJOY,* BRENDON! BUT THE ANSWER IS *YES!* WE CAN GO THROUGH AGAIN AS SOON AS THE *FIRE* DIES DOWN!

ALTHOUGH IT LOOKS TO ME LIKE THE DOORWAY IS *SHRINKING!* MAYBE WE SHOULDN'T WAIT *TOO* LONG— IT MAY NOT BE *STABLE!*

Umm... EXCUSE US, SIR...

WE DIDN'T MEAN TO *EAVES-DROP,* BUT...

...DID YOU SAY THAT YOU WANT TO GET BACK TO YOUR *MOTHER?*

DID YOU LEAVE HER IN THE MIDDLE OF A *WAR?*

HA HA HA HA HA! *KIDS!*

BLESS YOU, BOYS! IT HAS BEEN *TOO LONG* SINCE WE HAVE MET WITH SUCH *INNOCENCE!*

BUT TO ANSWER YOUR QUESTIONS, *OUR MOTHER* IS WHAT WE HUMANS CALL OUR HOME WORLD! AND YES, SHE *IS* AT *WAR...*

...WITH THE *MORG!* THEY ARE A VICIOUS, VIOLENT, *MONSTROUS* RACE WHO ARE DETERMINED TO *CONQUER* OUR MOTHER AND *ENSLAVE* ALL HUMANS!

THE MORG *DELIBERATELY* SET THE FOREST ON FIRE TO CAPTURE US! THE FOREST IS NOT *SACRED* TO THEM! *NOTHING* IS— EXCEPT *POWER!*

Hm... NOW I'M *SURE* THE DOORWAY IS SHRINKING!

THERE'S SOMETHING YOU'RE *NOT* TELLING US! WHAT'S SO *SPECIAL* ABOUT *YOU TWO* THAT ANYONE WOULD GO TO ALL THAT *TROUBLE?*

ME, I'M JUST A *WANDERING MAGICIAN* FROM THE EAST, BUT BRENDON *IS* SPECIAL! HE'S THE *LEADER*, THE *HERO*, THE *INSPIRATION*...

...FOR ALL *FREE* HUMANS ON OUR MOTHER! THE MORG WOULD GO TO A *GREAT DEAL* OF TROUBLE TO CAPTURE HIM! OR *KILL* HIM!

HINTER-MANN!

PLEASED TO *MEET* YOU, MR. BRENDON, SIR! IT'S A *SHAME* YOU HAVE TO BE *GOING* ALREADY, BUT I THINK I HEAR YOUR *MOTHER* CALLING!

GOODBYE! *GOODBYE!* WE'D OFFER TO HELP, BUT WE'RE KIND OF WRAPPED UP IN OUR OWN LITTLE *FAMILY* MATTER RIGHT NOW!

LISTEN! THAT HIGH-PITCHED *SCREECH!*

I *KNEW* IT! I JUST *KNEW* IT!

THOSE ARE *MORG WAR DRAGONS!*

WE'RE *REALLY* IN FOR IT NOW!

☠☀⚡🌀 *THIS* ISN'T *MORGWORLD!* THOSE HUMANS HAVE LED SNARK, NURG, AND GROOB SOME- PLACE ELSE! *WELL...*

GROOB DOESN'T CARE! GROOB HAS FOUND *BRENDON!* THE *REWARD* LORD MORAQ PROMISED FOR BREN- DON'S CAPTURE WILL SOON BE...

...GROOB'S!!

HINTERMANN! STAY HERE AND *GUARD* OUR NEW FRIENDS! I'LL *DRAW* THAT MORG WARRIOR *AWAY* FROM YOU!

YOU HEARD THE MAN! HIDE BEHIND THE *GOOFY* MAGICIAN!

WHIT! WHIT!

WHOOSH!

THUMP!

SKREEEEEEEE...

THUD!

13

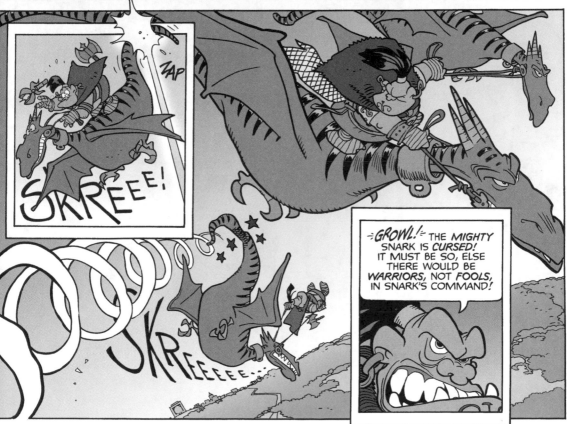

BUT NURG'S *RETRIBUTION* MUST *WAIT!* THE MAGIC DOORWAY IS *CLOSING,* AND NURG WILL NOT BE *STRANDED* IN THIS MISERABLE WORLD!

=GRRRR!= SNARK SAYS...

NO!!

POW!

NURG WILL LEAVE WHEN SNARK *ORDERS* NURG TO LEAVE! BUT FIRST SNARK HAS *BUSINESS* TO ATTEND TO!

SNARK KNOWS NOT *WHAT* THESE CREATURES ARE, BUT SNARK WILL BET CREATURES CAN BE *SOLD* IN THE *SLAVE MARKET* IN TOOM!

GROOB'S *WEAPONS* HAVE BEEN *TAKEN!* WHAT SHALL NURG DO TO *PUNISH* GROOB FOR THAT?

KICK!

LEAVE GROOB HERE! A MORG WARRIOR DEFEATED BY *HUMANS* HAS *NO VALUE!*

SOMETIMES, THERE'S A VERY FINE LINE BETWEEN REALITY AND FANTASY—

THANKS, DEWEY! I'D NEVER HAVE FIGURED OUT THIS PROBLEM WITHOUT *YOUR* HELP!

YOU'RE WELCOME, HUEY! IT'S FUN TO DO OUR HOMEWORK *TOGETHER!*

GOSH, UNCA DONALD— THAT'S QUITE A LOAD OF LAUNDRY! CAN WE *HELP?*

NO THANKS, LOUIE! YOU BOYS WORK *HARD ENOUGH* ALL DAY IN *SCHOOL!*

WHY DON'T YOU JUST RUN OUT TO THE *MOVIES* TONIGHT?

GOSH, UNCA DONALD! YOU'RE THE *BEST* UNCLE IN THE WORLD!

OUR *GENEROUS* UNCLE SCROOGE WILL BE HAPPY TO *PAY* FOR YOUR TICKETS AND YOUR POPCORN!

GOSH, *THANKS,* UNCA SCROOGE! YOU'RE THE *BEST* GRANDUNCLE IN THE WORLD!

TUT TUT, BOYS! WHAT'S THE USE OF HAVING *MONEY* IF YOU DON'T *SPEND* IT ON YOUR *LOVED ONES!*

WHOA! THAT *CAN'T* BE THE *REAL* UNCA SCROOGE!

Uh... WHAT HAPPENED? THE LAST THING I REMEMBER IS *ANOTHER* DREAM, ABOUT WARRIORS AND DRAGONS AND--

≈*ULP!*≈ THAT'S DEWEY AND LOUIE— *UNCONSCIOUS!*

19

WORLD OF THE DRAGONLORDS
CHAPTER 2: SLAVES OF THE MORG

II

GNAW!

MASTER CLARG! YOUR HUMBLE SLAVE RASMUS HAS BROUGHT THREE *NEW SLAVES!* THEY AWAIT YOUR COMMANDS!

CHOMP! SMACK! GNAW!

D/D 99002

PLEASE, SIR... CAN YOU TELL US WHAT HAPPENED TO OUR *UNCAS?* WE'RE AWFULLY *WORRIED!*

BURP!

SILENCE, SLAVE! STABLE-MASTER CLARG DOES *NOT* ANSWER QUESTIONS! CLARG GIVES *ORDERS...*

...AND *PUNISHES* SLAVES WHO DO NOT *INSTANTLY* OBEY!

SPLAT!

WHEN CLARG *CATCHES* THE INSULTER, CLARG WILL *RIP OUT* THE INSULTER'S *LIVER* AND EAT IT *RAW!*

Uh... *MASTER* CLARG? I... I SAW THE CHICKEN LEG *FALL* FROM A... Er... *PASSING DRAGON!*

A *WAR DRAGON?!*

≈AAARGH!≈ WHO DARES *INSULT* CLARG WITH *FOOD?!*

?!?

THEN... THE INSULTING OF CLARG WAS AN *ACCIDENT!*

IT.. IT *MUST* BE SO, ELSE CLARG WOULD HAVE TO DECLARE A *BLOOD FEUD* WITH A... A *DRAGON-LORD!*

RASMUS! CLARG ORDERS YOU TO PUT CLARG'S NEW STABLEBOYS TO *WORK!*

AS YOU COMMAND, MASTER!

CHOMP! CHOMP!..

THAT GREAT *OAF!* AS IF *HE'D* HAVE THE *COURAGE* TO CHALLENGE *ANYONE!*

DOES THAT MEAN WE DON'T HAVE TO *OBEY* HIM, RASMUS?

DON'T BE A *FOOL*, BOY! CLARG IS AN *EASY* MASTER BECAUSE HE'S TOO *LAZY* TO WHIP HIS SLAVES!

BUT IF YOU *DISPLEASE* HIM, HE'LL *SELL* YOU TO A MORG WHO'LL WHIP YOU JUST FOR *FUN*!

≈GULP!≈

REMEMBER, YOU BOYS ARE *PRISONERS* IN THE MORG FORTRESS OF *TOOM*! MORG *WARRIORS* ARE *EVERYWHERE*!

THERE'S *NO ESCAPE*, NO PLACE TO ESCAPE *TO*! THE MORG HAVE *CONQUERED* THE ENTIRE WORLD!

THAT'S *NOT* TRUE!

WHAT ABOUT THE *FREE* HUMANS?

WHAT ABOUT *BRENDON*?

≈GASP!≈ DON'T EVEN *MENTION* THAT NAME! IT'S *POISON* TO THE MORG!

FORGET ABOUT HIM, FORGET ABOUT YOUR *UNCLES*, FORGET ABOUT *EVERYTHING* EXCEPT WORKING HARD!

THE ONLY WAY TO *SURVIVE* IN TOOM IS TO *OBEY*!

MEANWHILE, BACK ON EARTH—

GUS GOOSE! DON'T YOU DARE TOUCH THAT PIE!

OR WOULD YOU LIKE ME TO GIVE YOU A BLAST OF ROCK SALT FROM ONE OF OLD BESSIE'S BARRELS?

N-N-NO, MUM!

COME ALONG, GUS! YOU'RE GOING BACK TO WORK!

Y-Y-YES, MUM! ≈OUCH!≈

CURSE SNARK AND NURG FOR LEAVING GROOB IN THIS MISERABLE WORLD WITHOUT WEAPONS!

BUT GROOB IS HUNGRY, AND GROOB DOES NOT NEED WEAPONS TO STEAL FOOD FROM AN OLD WOMAN!

≈YEEEE-OWCH!≈

BLAM!

AlEEEEE!

ZOOM!

LAND SAKES! ARE MY PIES SO GOOD THAT EVEN ALIEN VARMINTS ARE AFTER 'EM?!

≈GROAN!≈ I'M *EXHAUSTED!*

ME TOO! RASMUS HAS RUN US *RAGGED* FOR *HOURS!*

AT THIS RATE, WE'LL NEVER HAVE *TIME* TO LOOK FOR UNCA DONALD AND UNCA SCROOGE!

MUCH LESS FIGURE OUT HOW TO *ESCAPE!*

THAT'S TRUE— UNLESS WE *MAKE* TIME!

WE'RE ALL EARS, HUEY!

REMEMBER THAT *BOY* I TOLD YOU ABOUT? THE ONE WHO *BOMBED* CLARG? *HE* SEEMED TO BE MOVING ABOUT PRETTY *FREELY!*

AND LOOK AT ALL THE SLAVES RUSHING BACK AND FORTH— WHO CAN *TELL* IF THEY'RE ON *ERRANDS* FOR THEIR MASTERS OR *NOT?*

SO WHO'D KNOW IF ONE OF *US* TOOK OFF ON HIS *OWN?*

RASMUS, FOR ONE! HE'S SO AFRAID OF *CLARG* THAT HE COMES *LOOKING* FOR US IF HE EVEN *SUSPECTS* WE'RE GOOFING OFF!

Ah, BUT YOU'RE *FOR-GETTING* SOMETHING...

WE'RE *IDENTICAL TRIPLETS!*

SO FAR, SO *GOOD!* ASSUMING THAT DEWEY AND LOUIE REMEMBER TO CHECK IN AS *ME* FROM TIME TO TIME...

...I'LL HAVE THE REST OF THE DAY *FREE* TO LOOK AROUND FOR UNCA DONALD AND UNCA SCROOGE!

WAIT! THERE'S THAT *BOY* AGAIN!

GOOD *GRIEF!* IT'S CERTAINLY *OBVIOUS* THAT HE'S UP TO *NO GOOD!*

STILL, ANY *ENEMY* OF THE MORG COULD BE A *FRIEND* OF OURS! I'D BETTER *FOLLOW* HIM...

...NO MATTER ≶GULP!≶ *WHERE* HE LEADS!

Oh, MAN! MY *FEET* AREN'T REALLY *MADE* FOR *WALL CLIMBING!*

≠WHEW!≠ MADE IT!

BUT NOW WHERE DID THAT BOY GO?

≠GROAN!≠ WHAT IS HE— PART *MONKEY*? HE'S CROSS-ING OVER TO *ANOTHER* ROOF!

WELL, *PHOOEY* ON HIM! I DON'T HAVE TO *FOLLOW* TO KEEP AN *EYE* ON HIM!

Hm... WHAT'S HE DOING WITH THAT *PIGEON?!*

OHMIGOSH! IT'S A *CARRIER* PIGEON!

?

SOME SPY I AM! HE *KNEW* I WAS HERE ALL ALONG! I MIGHT AS WELL—

WAIT! UP IN THE *SKY!* THAT'S *NOT* THE PIGEON COMING BACK...

...IT'S A *MORG WAR DRAGON!* IT'S DIVING RIGHT AT THE *BOY,* BUT HE'S TOO BUSY SHOWING OFF TO *SEE* IT!

LOOK OUT!!!

KRUMPH!

SKREEE!

FWOOOOSHHH

29

≈UNGH!≈
≈UNNNGGH!≈

Oh, GIVE IT A REST, DONALD! YOU'LL *NEVER* SUCCEED IN *PULLING* OUR *CHAINS* OUT OF THE WALL!

≈GASP! GASP! GASP!≈

SAVE YOUR STRENGTH! YOU MAY *NEED* IT WHEN OUR CAPTORS *COME* FOR US!

BUT WHAT IF THEY *NEVER* COME, UNCLE SCROOGE? WHAT IF THEY'VE *THROWN* US IN HERE TO *ROT?*

THEY'LL *COME!* IF THEY WANTED TO DO AWAY WITH US, THEY WOULDN'T HAVE *WASTED* GOOD MONEY ON THESE *CHAINS!*

BUT WHAT ABOUT THE *BOYS?* I CAN'T JUST WAIT AROUND ON *YOUR* SAY SO! I'VE *GOT* TO GET FREE AND *RESCUE* THEM!

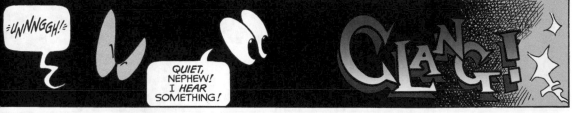

≈UNNNGGH!≈

QUIET, NEPHEW! I *HEAR* SOMETHING!

CLANG!

YES...

GENERAL HYRRR THINKS THESE STRANGE CREATURES WILL *INDEED* PLEASE LORD MORAQ!

AND BACK AT THE STABLES—

C'MON, HUEY... YOU'LL FEEL *BETTER* AFTER YOU'VE EATEN!

LOOK! WE MANAGED TO SCAVENGE THE *BEST SCRAPS* FROM CLARG'S DINNER TABLE!

THANKS, LOUIE, BUT I... I'M NOT HUNGRY! THERE'S JUST TOO *MUCH* TO *THINK* ABOUT!

YEAH! HOW TO FIND UNCA DONALD AND UNCA SCROOGE... HOW TO *ESCAPE*...

...HOW TO GET *HOME!*

THAT BOY...

SORRY TO RUIN YOUR *SOMBER* MOOD, BUT THAT "BOY" HAS A *NAME!*

SCRITCH!

IT'S *JUTE*, AND I'M GLAD TO SAY THAT HE'S STILL *VERY MUCH ALIVE!*

WHO... WHO ARE YOU?!

WHERE... WHERE DID YOU *COME* FROM?

I ALREADY TOLD YOU MY NAME— IT'S *JUTE!*

SUCH CURIOUS BOYS ARE *BOUND* TO HAVE *LOTS* OF OTHER QUESTIONS...

...BUT IF YOU *WANT* TO KNOW *MORE,* YOU'LL HAVE TO *FOLLOW ME!*

THIS *TUNNEL* IS PART OF A WHOLE *NETWORK* OF TUNNELS...

...THAT RUN BENEATH THE *ENTIRE* CITY OF TOOM! THEY WERE DUG *SECRETLY* BY HUMAN SLAVES!

THE MORG WOULD KILL US *ALL* IF THEY *DISCOVERED* THEM, SO BE *CAREFUL* AS YOU CLIMB OUT!

=GULP!=

Ah! WE'RE JUST IN *TIME!* HERE COMES THAT *FAT PIG* OF A STABLE MASTER, *CLARG!*

≈BURP!≈

IN TIME FOR *WHAT?!* TO GET CAUGHT AND *PUNISHED* BY THE MORG WHO *OWNS* US?!

IF THIS IS A *TRAP*, JUTE...

Oh, IT *IS!* BUT *NOT* FOR YOU THREE!

JUST HAVE A LITTLE *PATIENCE!*

WOW!

CLUNK!

SEE? THE SLAVES ALSO BUILT *FAKE* CHIMNEYS...

...ONTO MOST OF THE MORG BUILDINGS!

AND CRAWL SPACES *BETWEEN* EACH FLOOR, SO WE CAN *SPY* ON THE MORG, EVEN WHEN THEY *THINK* THEY'RE *ALONE!*

WOW AGAIN!

BUT WHAT'S THE *REASON* FOR ALL THAT CLOAK-AND-DAGGER WORK?

AND JUST WHO *PLANNED* IT ALL?!

≈SHH!≈ CLARG'S *BEDROOM* IS JUST BELOW! HE'LL ENTER ANY SECOND NOW!

WATCH! YOU'LL *LIKE* THIS!

≈YAWN!≈ CLARG HAS *WORKED* TOO *HARD* TODAY!

III

KA-RASH!

D/D99003

RASMUS!!!

≈HOO-HOO-HOO!≈ THE BEST PART IS THAT CLARG IS TOO *STUPID* TO FIGURE OUT THAT HIS BED *BROKE* BECAUSE...

≈SNICKER!≈

...I SNUCK IN EARLIER AND *SAWED* IT ≈HEE-HEE-HEE!≈ *ALMOST* IN PIECES!

HEY, *WAIT* JUST A DOGGONED MINUTE!

DON'T TELL US THE WHOLE *POINT* OF ALL THOSE SECRET TUNNELS AND PASSAGE-WAYS IS TO PLAY *PRACTICAL JOKES?!*

WE WANT SOME *ANSWERS,* MISTER!

AND WE WANT THEM *NOW!*

35

RASMUS! *RASMUS!* CLARG HEARD *VOICES* IN THE *CEILING!*

Hm... MAYBE *DRAGON-LORDS* LANDED ON THE *ROOF!* SHOULD I TELL THEM TO BE *QUIET?*

DRAGONLORDS?! NO, *NO!* CLARG L-L-L-*LIKES* HEARING VOICES!

Oh, MAN*!* THAT WAS *CLOSE!* LUCKY FOR US THAT RASMUS REMEMBERED HOW *SCARED* CLARG IS OF THE DRAGONLORDS!

IT'S TIME TO GET *SERIOUS,* JUTE!

WE WANT *ANSWERS* TO OUR QUESTIONS!

AND YOU'LL *GET* THEM— I *PROMISE!*

BUT... BUT THEN, WILL *YOU* ANSWER A QUESTION FOR *ME?*

IS... IS IT *TRUE* THAT YOU'VE MET *BRENDON?!*

—ELSEWHERE—

LORD MORAQ WILL CHOOSE *ONE* TO BE LORD MORAQ'S *PERSONAL* SLAVE! THE *OTHER* WILL BELONG TO GENERAL HYRRR!

GENERAL HYRRR THINKS THE DUCK CREATURE DOES *WELL* TO TREMBLE!

BAH! MORAQ IS AN OLD, *WEAK* FOOL WHO CANNOT *BEAR* TO EVEN *SEE* A HUMAN! THIS IS BECAUSE HUMANS *REMIND* MORAQ...

...OF MORAQ'S MANY *DEFEATS* AT THE HANDS OF *BRENDON!*

BUT ONCE *GENERAL HYRRR* IS IN *COMMAND* OF TOOM...!!!

!

37

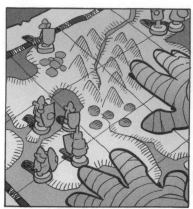

LORD MORAQ? GENERAL HYRRR HAS BROUGHT THE DUCK CREATURES!

IT MAKES LITTLE DIFFERENCE, BUT LORD MORAQ CHOOSES *THAT* ONE! TAKE THE OTHER AND *GO!*

LORD MORAQ IS IN THE MIDST OF PLANNING A *STRATEGY* TO DEFEAT BRE—

≈GRR!≈ THE *HUMAN.*

WHAP!

FIFTY ADDITIONAL DRAGONLORDS WILL ARRIVE *SOON!* THEN THE MORG WILL *ENCIRCLE* THE FREE HUMANS AND—

BAH! "STRATEGIES" ARE *NOT* THE *MORG* WAY! THE MORG ATTACK *HEAD-ON* AND *CRUSH* THE HUMANS' SKULLS!

WHAT?! DOES GENERAL HYRRR DARE *CHALLENGE* LORD MORAQ'S COMMAND?!

NOT... YET...

LORD MORAQ *THOUGHT* NOT!

NEXT MORNING—

=GROAN!= FEEDING THE DRAGONS IS A NEVER-ENDING JOB!

YOU SAID IT, BROTHER! THEY'RE ALWAYS HUNGRY!

Oh, I DON'T KNOW... I KIND OF LIKE FEEDING THEM! THEY'RE SO GRATEFUL THAT IT'S HARD TO REMEMBER...

...THAT THE MORG HAVE TRAINED THESE FRIENDLY VEGETARIANS TO BE TERRIFYING WAR BEASTS!

CHOMP! GOBBLE! SLURP!

=URK!=

UH-OH!

RRRUMBLE!

LOOK OUT! HE'S GONNA BLOW!

BURP!

FWOOSH!

YE CATS! HOW DID THE MORG EVER *TAME* THESE DRAGONS IN THE FIRST PLACE?!

ASK *JUTE*— IF YOU CAN GET A *STRAIGHT* ANSWER OUT OF HIM!

ARE YOU SAYING YOU DON'T *BELIEVE* WHAT HE TOLD US?

WELL....

"...I *BELIEVE* HIM WHEN HE SAID HE WAS ORPHANED AFTER THE MORG RAIDED HIS VILLAGE AND *ABDUCTED* HIM!"

"I GUESS I BELIEVE THAT HE *GREW UP* IN TOOM AS ONE OF *CLARG'S* SLAVES..."

"...AND THAT HE RAN *AWAY* WHEN HE "DISPLEASED" CLARG..."

"...WHICH MAKES IT *LIKELY* THAT HE HAS BEEN LIVING UNDER-GROUND EVER SINCE!"

BUT HE SURE WAS *EVASIVE* ABOUT EVERYTHING ELSE!

HE'S *HIDING* SOMETHING, BUT *WHAT?!*

WHAT'S THIS? SUSPICION? *DISTRUST*? ARE THEY THE *THANKS* I GET FOR BRINGING *NEWS* OF YOUR *UNCLES*?!

YOU'VE *FOUND* THEM?!

Um... NOT *EXACTLY*, BUT... BUT I'VE FOUND *SOMEONE* WHO WILL *KNOW* WHERE THEY ARE...

...THE MORG WARRIOR *NURG!* *HE'S* THE ONE WHO *SOLD* YOU TO CLARG!

Oh... ÷SIGH!÷ HE WON'T TALK TO *US!*

NO, BUT I ALSO FOUND OUT THAT HE'S *CHALLENGED* ANOTHER MORG NAMED *SNARK* TO *COMBAT* OVER THE *SPOILS* OF THEIR LAST RAID!

THE SPOILS INCLUDE YOUR *UNCLES!* LET'S GO *WATCH*— MAYBE ONE OF THE MORG WILL *SAY* SOMETHING DURING THE FIGHT!

HOLD ON! WE CAN'T *ALL* GO!

CLARG MAY BE AN *IDIOT*, BUT *RASMUS* IS A REAL *SLAVE DRIVER!*

YEAH, HE'LL *NOTICE* IF WE'RE *ALL* GONE, AND *PUNISH* US!

BUT... BUT...

NEVER MIND! I'LL TAKE JUST *DEWEY!* WE DON'T HAVE *TIME* TO ARGUE! THE *CHALLENGE*...

"...IS ABOUT TO START!"

C'MON! WE'LL NEVER BE ABLE TO SEE OVER THAT RING OF WARRIORS, AND WE CAN'T GET THROUGH IT!

BUT WE CAN GET A GOOD VIEW FROM ATOP THIS PILE OF ALE JUGS!

≈GROAN!≈ NOW I SEE WHY HUEY CALLED YOU PART MONKEY!

DON'T YOU HAVE A SECRET VIEW-PORT IN A NICE, SOLID BUILDING?

TOO MANY MORG AROUND TO RISK USING IT!

SNARK HAS CHEATED NURG! NOW NURG DEMANDS VENGEANCE!

THE MIGHTY SNARK LAUGHS AT THE WEAK-LING NURG!

AARR!

GH!...

CRUMP!

CLONK!

HEE-YAAH!

SNARK *WINS* AGAIN! LIKE WHEN SNARK DID WHEN SNARK SOLD THE *LARGE DUCK CREATURES* TO *LORD MORAQ!*

THUMP!

NOW I KNOW WHERE YOUR UNCLES ARE! C'MON!

BOY! GAK HAS *NEED* OF A NEW SQUIRE!

TELL GAK WHO BOY'S *MASTER* IS SO GAK CAN *BUY BOY!*

Uh.... Er... GULP!

Uh-oh! THAT MORG WILL FIND OUT JUTE IS A *RUNAWAY SLAVE!* BUT THE ONLY THING I CAN *DO...*

43

RUMMBLE!

≠GAK!≠

...IS TO START AN *AVALANCHE!!!*

CLUMSY SLAVE! GAK WILL *WHIP* SLAVE *SENSELESS* FOR THIS!

WAIT! THE BOY IS *STABLE-MASTER CLARG'S* SLAVE!

MASTER CLARG *DELIGHTS* IN WHIPPING HIS SLAVES *PERSONALLY!*

≠HMPH!≠ AS LONG AS SLAVE IS *PUNISHED!*

RASMUS, I... I...

QUIET, DEWEY! I'M CERTAINLY *NOT* GOING TO LET CLARG WHIP YOU FOR SAVING JUTE'S LIFE!

IT WOULDN'T BE *PROPER* FOR THE *LEADER* OF THE HUMAN *RESISTANCE* IN TOOM TO TURN *ANYONE* OVER TO A *MORG!*

ESPECIALLY NOT HIS *NEWEST RECRUIT!*

BRENDON

To prepare for illustrating *World of the Dragonlords*, Giorgio Cavazzano worked closely with Byron Erickson in fully fleshing out the characters. On these pages, and others throughout the book, we're pleased to reproduce a number of Cavazzano's preliminary sketches.

BRENDON
An early model study of Brendon (the leader of the humans). It was ultimately decided that he would be clean-shaven.

HINTERMANN
A model study of Hintermann (the human magician).

FWOOSH!

JUTE

JUTE
*A model study of Jute
(the stable boy).*

SILIA
A model study of Silia.

UNCLE SCROOGE

A model study of Scrooge as Lord Moraq's personal slave and General Hyrrr's advisor

DONALD DUCK

A model study of Donald as a slave.

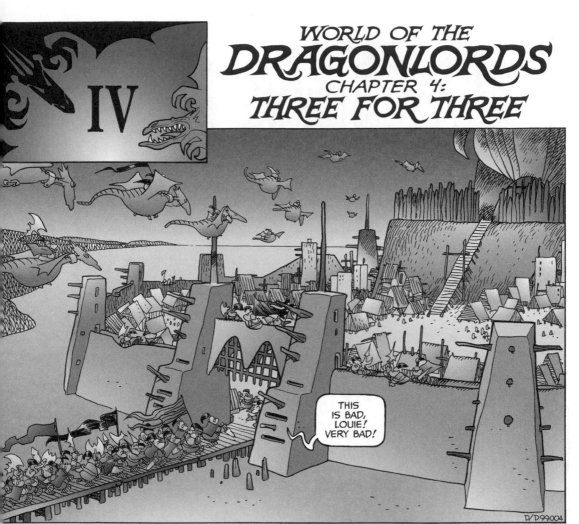

THIS IS BAD, LOUIE! VERY BAD!

D/D99004

EVEN *WORSE*, RASMUS SAYS THESE TROOPS ARE ONLY THE *BEGINNING* OF THE *REINFORCEMENTS* LORD MORAQ HAS ORDERED!

WHEN THEY ALL ARRIVE, THE MORG ARMY IN TOOM WILL CONSIST OF *75 DRAGONLORDS* AND *500 FOOT SOLDIERS*...

...ALL DEDICATED TO *WIPING OUT* BRENDON'S FREE HUMANS!

49

BUT SURELY THE *RESISTANCE* CAN DO SOMETHING TO *SABOTAGE* THE MORG ARMY?

WELL...

I MEAN, *THAT'S* GOT TO BE THE *POINT* OF ALL YOUR SECRET TUNNELS, RIGHT?

OF COURSE! BUT NOT THE *WHOLE* POINT!

YOU SEE, RESISTANCE SLAVES ARE ALSO DIGGING A TUNNEL *UNDERNEATH* THE WALLS OF TOOM!

"WHEN IT'S *FINISHED*, BRENDON WILL LEAD HIS BAND OF FREE HUMANS THROUGH IT..."

"...JOIN UP WITH THE *RESISTANCE*..."

...AND ATTACK THE MORG, CATCHING THEM COMPLETELY OFF GUARD!"

THE WHOLE PLAN WAS *BRENDON'S* IDEA! GOSH— ISN'T HE *WONDERFUL?*

I'VE NEVER *MET* HIM, BUT I *REPORT* TO HIM ABOUT THE TUNNEL'S *PROGRESS*— BY *CARRIER PIGEON!*

LUCKY YOU...

IF WE *DUCKS* ARE JUST AS LUCKY, WE'LL FIND OUR UNCLES AND *ESCAPE* BEFORE THE BATTLE EVEN *STARTS!*

OH... YEAH... IT'S NOT *YOUR* FIGHT!

BUT LISTEN! I ALREADY FOUND OUT YOUR UNCLES ARE IN *LORD MORAQ'S FORTRESS,* RIGHT?

WELL, FINDING A *SAFE PASSAGE* FOR THEM *OUT* OF IT WILL BE *TRICKY,* BUT I'LL *LOOK* FOR ONE AS SOON AS I TAKE YOU BACK TO THE STABLES!

IN THE MEANTIME, JUST THINK OF *CLARG'S* FAT FACE WHEN HE REALIZES HE'LL HAVE TO TAKE ORDERS FROM *ME!*

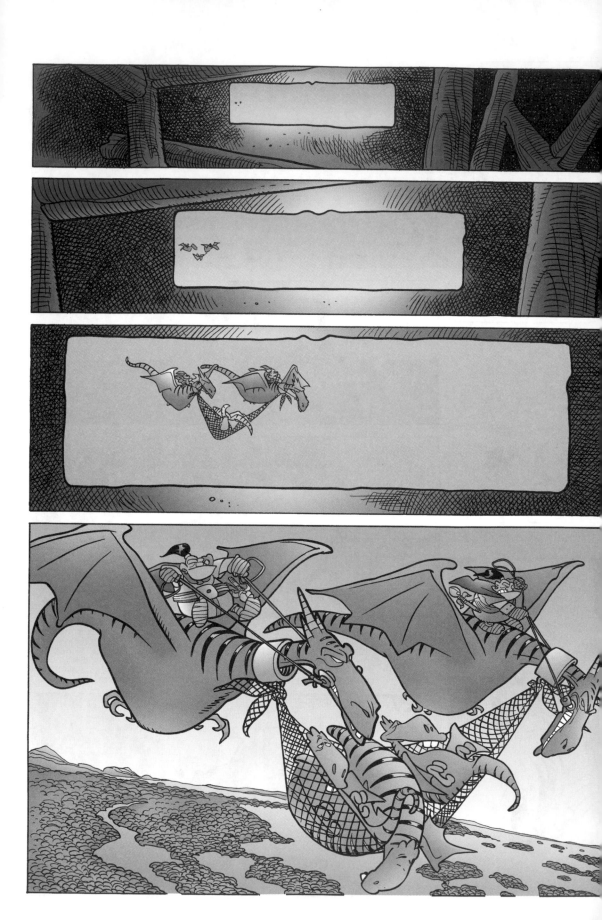

GOOD! DO NOT *CROSS* HYRRR, SLAVE!

D-D-DON'T YOU WORRY, BOSS! I'LL HAVE THESE STONES *CLEAN AND SHINY* IN NO TIME!

BUT... uh... *BOSS?* WILL YOU LEAVE THE DOOR *OPEN?* IT'S KINDA HARD TO *SEE* IN TORCHLIGHT!

=*GRRRR!*=

VERY WELL! GENERAL HYRRR WILL *GRANT* SLAVE'S REQUEST!

THANKS, BOSS!

Hm... THIS TAR IS PRETTY *STICKY* STUFF...

...BUT I'M BEGINNING TO MAKE A *LITTLE* PROGRESS!

?

ZZT!

ZZT!

=*GLEEP!*=

ZZT!

HA-HA-HA-HA-HA! SLAVE DID NOT KNOW THAT *SUNLIGHT* IS WHAT *CHARGES* LIGHTNING STONES!

ZZAP!

=*OUCH!*=

ZZAP!

=*OUCH!*=

ZZAP!

=*OUCH!*=

ZZT!

—LSEWHERE—

YE CATS! THE STABLES HAVE DESCENDED INTO *CHAOS!*

SKREEEEE...

SKREEEE... ZZAP!

STUPID BEAST! SKREEE SKREEÈ

LOUIE! THERE YOU ARE! WHERE HAVE YOU **BEEN?**

JUTE AND I WERE—

NEVER MIND! I DON'T HAVE **TIME** TO HEAR IT!

AS YOU CAN SEE, IT'S A **MADHOUSE** AROUND HERE! THE SLAVES ARE **SCARED,** THE NEW MORG ARE **SURLY...**

...AND **CLARG** IS HAVING AN **APOPLECTIC FIT!**

HE'S **ORDERED** ME TO ASSIGN YOU BOYS TO OUR **LATEST** ARRIVALS!

Huh? BUT—

THERE'S NO TIME, **NO TIME!** YOUR **BROTHERS** ARE IN THERE— **THEY'LL** EXPLAIN!

SKREE!

≈KOFF! KOFF!≈

AND ON A DIFFERENT WORLD—

WE'RE IN *BIG* TROUBLE, LOUIE! CLARG MADE US PERSONALLY *RESPONSIBLE* FOR THOSE BABY DRAGONS!

HE SAID THEY'RE EXTREMELY *VALUABLE*, AND THREATENED TO *SKIN US ALIVE* IF ANYTHING *HAPPENS* TO THEM!

BUT *"SPITFIRE"* THERE...

...AND *"SMOKY"* OVER THERE...

...WON'T EVEN LET US GET *NEAR* THEIR BROTHER!

WHAT IF HE'S *BADLY HURT?!*

ONE THING'S FOR SURE— CLARG WILL BLAME *US* IF HE DIES!

POOR LITTLE GUY...

IF ONLY THERE WAS SOME WAY WE COULD *REVIVE* HIM!

Hm... MAYBE THERE *IS!*

THIS *CAULIFLOWER* IS PRETTY *SMELLY* STUFF!

SO IF I CAN WAVE IT UNDER THE UNCONSCIOUS BABY'S *NOSE...!!!*

THAT'S WHERE *YOU TWO* COME IN! YOU'LL HAVE TO *DISTRACT* SPITFIRE AND SMOKY!

=GULP!=

Oh, *BROTHER!* THE THINGS WE DO TO *SAVE OUR SKINS...!*

SNIF SNIF

MEANWHILE, IN THE FORTRESS KITCHEN—

GREAT! AT LAST I GOT A LEAD ON THE *WHEREABOUTS* OF *UNCLE SCROOGE!*

IT'S JUST TOO BAD THE ONLY PASSAGE I COULD FIND IS THIS *GARBAGE CHUTE!* IT'S TOO *SMALL* TO SMUGGLE OUT A FULL-GROWN—

NO!!!

CLANG

LORD MORAQ *HAS* DECIDED THAT GENERAL HYRRR MAY *NOT* WELCOME THE NEW WARRIORS!

!

BUT AS THE HIGHEST RANK-ING GENERAL IN TOOM, IT IS GENERAL HYRRR'S *PRIVILEGE* TO—

NO! LORD MORAQ WILL *PERSONALLY* ACCEPT THE NEW WARRIORS *OATH* OF FEALTY!

BESIDES, LORD MORAQ DOES NOT WANT GENERAL HYRRR TO *POISON* MORE MINDS WITH TALK OF *HEAD-ON ASSAULTS* ON THE HUMANS!

LORD MORAQ'S *ENCIRCLEMENT* STRATEGY IS LAID, AND IT *WILL NOT CHANGE!*

THEN *WHAT... IS LEFT...* FOR *GENERAL HYRRR...* TO *COMMAND?!*

BAH! GENERAL HYRRR IS NOT *FIT* TO COMMAND *MORG WARRIORS!*

BUT GENERAL HYRRR HAS *PERMISSION* TO COMMAND *SLAVE* TO CLEAN UP THIS MESS!

SLAM

GENERAL HYRRR WAS *RIGHT*— LORD MORAQ *IS A FOOL!*

I MEAN, JUST *LOOK* AT WHAT LORD MORAQ CALLS HIS "ENCIRCLEMENT STRATEGY"!

NOW IT'S TRUE, I DON'T KNOW THE *SCALE* OF THIS MAP, BUT UNLESS WE'RE TALKING ABOUT AN AREA OF ONLY A *FEW* SQUARE MILES...

...MORAQ WOULD NEED *TEN TIMES* AS MANY WARRIORS AS HE'LL HAVE TO *COMPLETELY* ENCIRCLE THE HUMAN CAMP!

EVEN IF HE *SUCCEEDED*, THE HUMAN REBELS ARE *GUERRILLA* FIGHTERS! THEY COULD EASILY *SNEAK THROUGH* THE MORG LINES...

...STAGE HIT-AND-RUN *ATTACKS*, AND *DISAPPEAR* BACK INTO THE FOREST!

NO, THE ONLY *WORKABLE* STRATEGY IS *YOURS*— ATTACK *HEAD*-ON AND *CRUSH* THE HUMANS' SKULLS!

SRAP!

≈GASP!≈ HERE I *FINALLY* FIND ONE OF THE BOYS' *UNCLES*...

...AND IT TURNS OUT HE'S *HELPING* THE MORG!

SPLENDID! SPLENDID! *SPLENDID!*

D/D 2000-001

CLARG HAS DONE *CLARG'S* PART AND DELIVERED THE DRAGON BABIES IN *GOOD* CONDITION!

BUT CAN TRAINER SKAG DO *SKAG'S* PART AND TRAIN SUCH *YOUNG* DRAGONS?!

YANK!

AYE!

65

ALL *HAPPY* TO *PUNISH* REBELLIOUS DRAGONS AND INTERFERING SLAVES...

...NOT TO MENTION IDIOTIC *STABLE-MASTERS!*

R-R-RASMUS! P-P-PUT THE DRAGON BABIES B-B-BACK IN THE STABLE!

YES, MASTER CLARG!

AND *LOCK UP* THOSE BOYS! CLARG CAN'T *RISK* THAT BOYS WILL *ANGER* TRAINER SKAG AGAIN!

AND THEN BRING CLARG *ALE!* *LOTS* OF ALE!

ENOUGH TO *DROWN* YOU, YOU *BESOTTED* OAF!

RASMUS, DO WE *HAVE* TO TURN THE BABIES OVER TO *SKAG?*

WE CAN TRAIN THEM MUCH *BETTER* THAN HE CAN!

TRUE! I'VE *SEEN* YOU WITH THEM! THEY OBEY YOU BECAUSE YOU TREAT THEM WITH *KINDNESS!*

SNIFF!

ELSEWHERE— AT LAST! IT TOOK ALL NIGHT, BUT I FINALLY FOUND "UNCA" DONALD!

CLAK!

WELL, WHADDAYA KNOW? IT *WORKS!*

ONLY... ONLY WHAT'S HE *DOING?!*

NEPHEW! YOU IN THERE?

KNOCK! KNOCK!

UNCLE SCROOGE?!

NO! DON'T OPEN THE...

ZZT! ZZT!

ZZAP!

ZZAP!

ZZAP!

...DOOR!

ZZAP!

GOOD GRIEF, NEPHEW! WHAT WAS *THAT* ALL ABOUT?!

SLAM!

≈GROAN!≈ I... I WAS TRYING TO MAKE A... *MACHINE GUN* OUT OF THE MORG'S LIGHTNING STONES...

...SO I COULD *BLAST* MY WAY OUT OF HERE AND *RESCUE THE BOYS!*

≈HMPH!≈ AND NO DOUBT GET YOURSELF *KILLED* IN THE PROCESS!

MAYBE SO, BUT I'VE GOT TO DO *SOMETHING!* THE LITTLE TYKES ARE PROBABLY *SCARED STIFF!*

BESIDES, IT'S MY *DUTY* AS *HEAD* OF *THE FAMILY!*

≈SIGH!≈ MUCH AS I HATE TO *ADMIT* IT, I'M THE HEAD OF OUR FAMILY, AND I'M *ALREADY* DOING SOMETHING!

BY *SUCKING UP* TO GENERAL HYRRR, I'VE LEARNED THAT THE BOYS ARE *SAFE* FOR NOW— IN THE *STABLES!*

!

I'VE ALSO SET AN *ESCAPE PLAN* IN MOTION, BUT IT'LL TAKE TIME TO—

IF ONLY THERE WAS SOME WAY WE COULD *CONTACT* THE BOYS!

WELL, I COULD TAKE A *MESSAGE* TO THEM...

?

?!

...OR YOU COULD *FOLLOW ME* AND DELIVER IT TO THEM *IN PERSON!*

BUT—

...YOUR UNCLE SCROOGE *REFUSED* TO COME WITH ME!

HE WOULDN'T LET YOUR UNCLE DONALD COME *EITHER!*

HE SAID HIDING IN TUNNELS WOULDN'T GET YOU *HOME*, BUT THAT HIS *PLAN* EVENTUALLY *WOULD*— IF IT *WORKS!*

HE WOULDN'T TELL YOU WHAT HIS PLAN *IS?*

NO, AND HE WOULDN'T TELL YOUR *UNCLE DONALD,* EITHER! MAN, WHAT AN *ARGUMENT* THAT STARTED!

SOME *FAMILY* YOU BOYS HAVE! *DESPITE* THEIR... ER... *QUIRKS,* I COULD... *FEEL* THAT THEY BOTH *CARE* FOR YOU!

YEAH, GOOD OL' UNCA DONALD...

=SIGH!=

GOOD OL' UNCA SCROOGE...

IT'S TOO BAD THEY *DIDN'T* COME WITH YOU JUTE! IT WOULD HAVE BEEN NICE TO SAY *GOOD-BYE!*

YOU SEE...

...WE'VE DECIDED TO *LEAVE TOOM* TONIGHT!

WHAT?!!

WHY?! HOW?!

THE "WHY" IS *EASY!*

SKAG WANTS TO START *"TRAINING"* THE BABY DRAGONS *TOMORROW!*

WE *CAN'T* LET THAT HAPPEN! WE JUST *CAN'T!*

SNIFF!

AT FIRST, WE PLANNED TO JUST *RELEASE* THE BABIES!

BUT CLARG WOULD KNOW *WE* DID IT...

...AND SKIN US ALIVE— OR *WORSE!*

SO TONIGHT, AS SOON AS TOOM IS *ASLEEP...*

...WE'LL CLIMB ONTO THE BACKS OF THE BABIES...

...AND *FLY* THEM OVER THE WALLS— TO *FREEDOM!*

GASP!

OUR PLAN IS TO FIND *BRENDON'S* CAMP AND HIDE OUT THERE!

THEN, WHEN THE *TUNNEL* UNDER THE WALLS IS FINISHED...

...WE'LL *JOIN* THE RAID ON TOOM AND *FREE* OUR UNCLES!

HA! *INSANITY* MUST RUN IN YOUR *FAMILY!* YOU BOYS ARE EVEN *CRAZIER* THAN YOUR UNCLES!

YOU'LL *NEVER* BE ABLE TO *FIND* BRENDON'S CAMP ON YOUR *OWN*, YOU KNOW!

AND WHAT ABOUT *RASMUS?!* THE MORG WILL THINK HE *HELPED* YOU ESCAPE!

OH, YEAH... CLARG ORDERED HIM TO *LOCK US IN!*

EXACTLY! THEY'LL QUICKLY PUT AN *END* TO HIM— AND IT WILL BE *YOUR* FAULT!

BUT *CHEER UP!* THOSE ARE JUST *DETAILS* I CAN HELP YOU *IRON OUT!*

MEANWHILE, BACK ON EARTH—

I STILL DON'T LIKE THAT NEW KID, SHARLA!

Oh, GROOB'S ALL RIGHT...

...ALTHOUGH HIS TABLE MANNERS ARE ATROCIOUS!

=CHOMP!=
=SLURP!=
=GULP!=

HONK! HONK! HONK!

GROOB IS STILL HUNGRY! DO CHILDREN HAVE MORE DOG HOT FOOD?!

HEY! IT'S PETE!

MAN, AM I GLAD I FOUND YOU GUYS!

SCREECH!

RAMBLIN' STUDIOS IS HOLDING OPEN AUDITIONS FOR EXTRAS IN GALACTIC DOOM!

THE KIDS WHO WON THE PARTS NEVER SHOWED UP!

ALL RIGHT! IT'S OUR BIG CHANCE!

WAIT TILL YOU SEE THE NEW KID WE MET, PETE! HIS COSTUME WILL WOW THE CASTING DIRECTOR!

GOSH! IT LOOKS LIKE HE'S FAINTED!?!

LATE THAT NIGHT, BACK IN TOOM—

RASMUS!

RASMUS!

RASMUS ⸝HIC!⸜ CLARG NEEDS MORE ALE!

BLAM!

JUTE!!!

SORRY, CLARG, BUT YOUR LACKEY IS "OUT" FOR THE NIGHT!

I HATED TO COLD-COCK HIM, BUT HE KEPT REFUSING TO GIVE ME HIS KEYS!

CLARG WILL CRUSH REBELLIOUS BOY!

AH-AH-AH! FIRST YOU'LL HAVE TO CATCH ME!

CLARG WILL CATCH JUTE...

...AND THEN CLARG WILL CRUSH—

AAGH!

PLOTCH!

YAHOO!!

YIPPEE!!

!!!

...THE *REASON* I STOLE RASMUS' KEYS!

HEY, LOOK AT CLARG'S FACE! HE LOOKS LIKE HE'S ABOUT TO *CRY*!

CLARG IS *D-D-D-DOOMED!* *CLARG* WILL BE CRUSHED AS SOON AS LORD MORAQ HEARS THAT BABY DRAGONS HAVE *ESCAPED!*

CLARG WILL CRUSH JUTE *LATER!* BUT FIRST...

...CLARG WILL MAKE SURE BABY DRAGONS DO *NOT* ESCAPE!

79

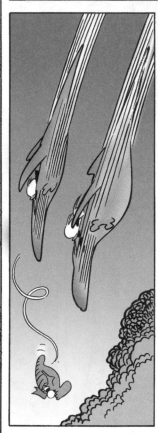

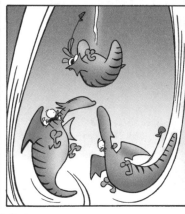

SNIFFLES, SOMETHING TELLS ME THIS *ISN'T* THE FIRST TIME YOUR BROTHERS HAVE DONE THIS!

SNIF!

AW, DON'T BE *EMBARRASSED,* BOY! THAT'S WHAT *FAMILIES* ARE FOR— TO *HELP* EACH OTHER!

I JUST WISH YOU COULD *UNDERSTAND* ME! IF YOU COULD, I'M CERTAIN YOU'D HELP ME HELP *MY* FAMILY!

CHOMP!

WHOOSH!!!

SKREE!

SKREE!

SKREE!

SKREEEEE!

HOLY COW! WHERE... WHAT... WHO?!

WELL, UNLESS I MISS MY GUESS, THAT'S THEIR MAMA!

MEANWHILE, BACK IN TOOM—

NAY, GENERAL HYRRR! *FOOL CLARG* DID NOT RAISE THE *ALARM* IN TIME!

REPORT! DID SNARK'S PATROL *CATCH* THE BABY DRAGONS?

IT IS NOT *CLARG'S* FAULT! GENERAL HYRRR SHOULD BLAME THE *WICKED* STABLE BOY, *JUTE!*

OR BLAME *SNARK!* IT WAS *SNARK* WHO SOLD THE *OTHER* WICKED STABLE BOYS TO CLARG!

GRRR...

ENOUGH! GENERAL HYRRR BLAMES *CLARG!* AND SO WILL LORD MORAQ!

NO! NO! CLARG BEGS FOR *MERCY!* CLARG DOES NOT *WANT* TO BE *CRUSHED!*

MERCY? THAT IS NOT A *MORG* WORD!

SAY IT!

WAIT! CLARG'S SLAVE HAS JUST *REMINDED* CLARG OF... OF WHO IS *REALLY* TO BLAME!

THE B-B-BLAME ⸗GULP!⸗ BELONGS TO THE WEAK AND... AND COWARDLY *L-L-LORD MORAQ!*

IF... IF *GENERAL HYRRR* RULED *TOOM* INSTEAD OF LORD MORAQ, NO SLAVE WOULD *DARE* REVOLT! ALL SLAVES *FEAR* GENERAL HYRRR!

⸗GASP!⸗ *TREASON!*

CLARG MUST BE *MAD!*

AYE... CLARG *MUST* BE MAD, BUT THERE IS *TRUTH* IN EVEN WHAT A *MADMAN* SAYS!

⸗WHIMPER!⸗

THAT IS WHY GENERAL HYRRR *ORDERS* THAT LAST NIGHT'S DEEDS BE KEPT *SECRET* FROM LORD MORAQ!

AGREED?!

AYE! SNARK SMELLS A *CHALLENGE* TO LORD MORAQ IN THE WIND...

...AND SNARK KNOWS THAT THE *VICTOR* WILL HAVE MANY *SPOILS* TO DIVIDE!

SOME *NEST* YOU'VE GOT HERE, SNIFFLES! NOW I UNDERSTAND WHY YOU BABIES HEADED FOR THE MOUNTAIN ...IT'S YOUR *HOME!*

SOME *MAMA* YOU'VE GOT, TOO! I'M STILL NOT SURE SHE *TRUSTS* US DUCKS...

...BUT AT LEAST SHE LET US "COME OVER AND *PLAY!*"

HEY, LOUIE! CHECK IT OUT!

EVER SINCE WE GOT HERE, THE BABIES ARE *EASY* TO CONTROL!

WE CAN TEACH THEM *TRICKS,* TOO! WATCH...

...I'VE TAUGHT SMOKY TO DO A *POWER CLIMB!*

87

AND I'VE TAUGHT SPITFIRE HOW TO DO A *"LOOP-THE-LOOP"!*

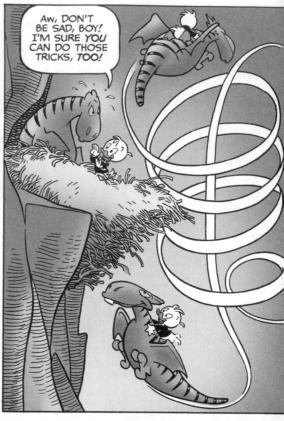

AW, *DON'T* BE SAD, BOY! I'M SURE *YOU* CAN DO THOSE TRICKS, *TOO!*

BUT FIRST YOU HAVE TO *REST* A BIT... RECOVER YOUR *STRENGTH!*

SNIF!

SUGAR CUBES! PACKED FULL OF RAW *ENERGY!*

AND I'VE GOT JUST WHAT YOU *NEED* RIGHT HERE IN MY FOOD BAG!

BACK IN TOOM AGAIN—

ARE YOU *SURE* YOUR REBELS WILL *WELCOME* MY NEPHEWS ONCE THEY GET THERE?

RELAX! THEY'LL BE PERFECTLY *SAFE* IN FREEDOM MARSH...

...UNLESS ONE OF THEM *FALLS OFF* HIS DRAGON!

WHAT?!

BUT *DON'T WORRY* ABOUT IT! THE BOYS ARE ALREADY *EXPERT* DRAGONRIDERS!

YOU KNOW, I'M NOT SURE I *LIKE* YOU...

YEAH? WHAT'S WITH THE *NEW OUTFIT?* THINKING OF GOING *NATIVE?*

NO... IT'S JUST THAT I'VE HAD A FEW ÷OOG!÷ *ACCIDENTS...*

OKAY, OKAY, I'VE HAD A *LOT* OF ACCIDENTS! ESPECIALLY *TODAY,* AFTER UNCLE SCROOGE MADE *ME* RESPONSIBLE FOR PART OF HIS *SECRET PLAN!*

HE WANTS ME TO *SABOTAGE* ALL THE MORG WEAPONS IN THIS ARMORY, BUT YOU KNOW WHAT?

SOME OF THESE WEAPONS ARE DOGGONED *SHARP!*

÷SNICKER!÷

89

ISN'T THAT AN *AMAZING* SIGHT?!

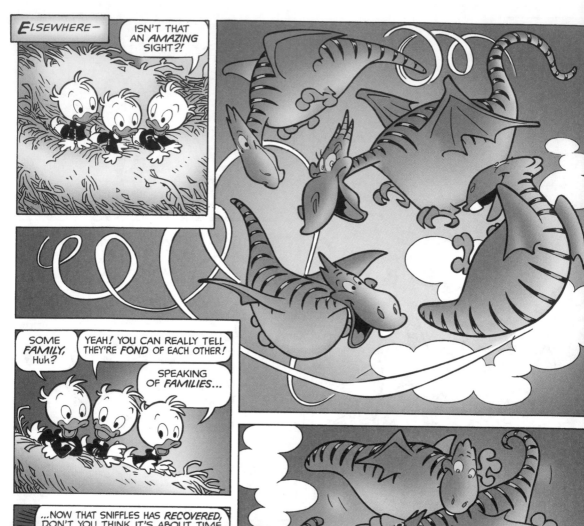

SOME *FAMILY,* Huh?

YEAH! YOU CAN REALLY TELL THEY'RE *FOND* OF EACH OTHER!

SPEAKING OF *FAMILIES...*

...NOW THAT SNIFFLES HAS *RECOVERED,* DON'T YOU THINK IT'S ABOUT TIME WE GET ON WITH THE BUSINESS OF *RESCUING OURS?*

WELL, YES, BUT...

...I THINK WE NEED TO *CHANGE* OUR PLAN!

I MEAN, WE JUST *CAN'T* BREAK UP THAT *HAPPY FAMILY* AGAIN, CAN WE?

NO...

SO WE'LL HAVE TO *CLIMB DOWN* THIS MOUNTAIN AND *WALK* TO FREEDOM MARSH!

YOU'RE RIGHT! IT SHOULDN'T TAKE MORE THAN A *FEW DAYS*...

LET'S GET STARTED WHILE THE DRAGONS ARE *BUSY!* I CAN'T *BEAR* TO SAY GOODBYE TO SPITFIRE!

...SKREEEE.

SKREE

91

WELL, I'LL *BE!* IT... IT'S LIKE MAMA'S GIVING US *PERMISSION* TO BORROW HER SONS!

SKREE!

YES! SHE *IS!*

NEXT STOP, *FREEDOM MARSH!*

YAHOO!!!

LORD MORAQ
*A model study of Lord Moraq
(the Morg commander).*

A model study of a Morg warrior.

Model studies of captive dragon with saddle, reins, and a Morg rider.

GENERAL HYRRR & UNCLE SCROOGE

A model study of Scrooge as Lord Moraq's personal slave and General Hyrrr's "advisor."

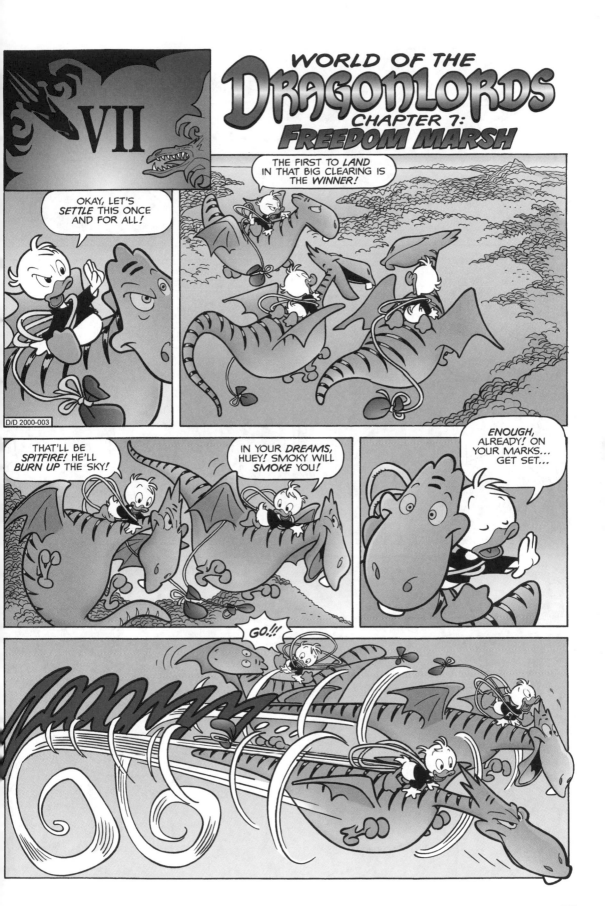

FASTER, SMOKY! FASTER! HUEY WILL *GLOAT* FOREVER IF HE WINS!

TOO LATE, *SLOWPOKE!* I'VE ALREADY...

...WON?

THE MORG?

LISTEN, GUYS! MAYBE WE SHOULD KNOCK OFF THE *SIBLING RIVALRY* FOR A WHILE!

I MEAN, FUN'S FUN, BUT WE *ARE* IN A *WAR ZONE!*

YOU KNOW, JUTE *TOLD US* ABOUT THE MORG'S *SCORCHED-EARTH* TACTICS...

...BUT ACTUALLY *SEEING* THE RESULTS IS PRETTY *SOBERING!*

WHAT DO YOU SUPPOSE HAPPENED TO THE *VILLAGERS?*

MEANWHILE, BACK ON EARTH—

I'M *WORRIED SICK!* DONALD AND THE BOYS HAVE BEEN *MISSING* FOR FAR TOO LONG!

RELAX, DAISY...

LOOK ON THE *BRIGHT SIDE*— NOW DONALD CAN'T PESTER YOU TO GO *BOWLING!*

GLADSTONE!!!

SIT DOWN, GROOB! YOU'RE *EMBARRASSING* US!

ER... I MEAN... THEY'RE PROBABLY JUST OFF ON ANOTHER *TREASURE HUNT* WITH UNCLE SCROOGE!

GEEZ! YOU'D THINK HE'S NEVER SEEN A *BIG CITY* BEFORE!

MAYBE HE *HASN'T!*

I DON'T THINK GROOB'S FROM AROUND HERE, MERVIE! IN FACT, I THINK HE'S A *FOREIGNER!*

YEAH, WELL HE *ACTS* LIKE AN *ALIEN!*

≈SIGH!≈ I JUST WISH I HAD SOME KIND OF *CLUE* TO WHERE DONALD AND THE BOYS WENT!

AND ON ANOTHER WORLD—

I DON'T GET IT— WE SHOULD HAVE REACHED *FREEDOM MARSH* BY NOW!

ARE YOU SAYING WE'RE *LOST?*

Uh... THAT'S JUST IT— I DON'T *KNOW!* JUTE'S DIRECTIONS WEREN'T EXACTLY *EXACT!*

YEAH! ALL HE SAID WAS "FLY EAST-NORTHEAST FOR A COUPLE OF HOURS UNTIL YOU GET TO A LARGE *MARSH*"!

HE... HE MADE IT SOUND SO *EASY!*

I'M GOING TO CLIMB HIGH ENOUGH TO GET A GOOD *OVERVIEW* OF THE TERRAIN!

MAYBE I'LL GET *LUCKY* AND SPOT A *MARSH* IN THE DISTANCE!

≈OOF!≈ WHAT'S THE *BIG IDEA,* SPITFIRE?!

SKREEE

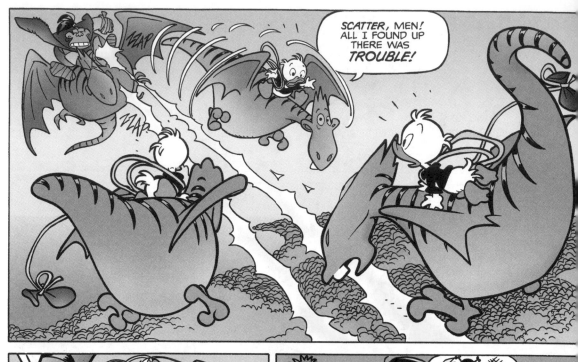

SCATTER, MEN! ALL I FOUND UP THERE WAS *TROUBLE!*

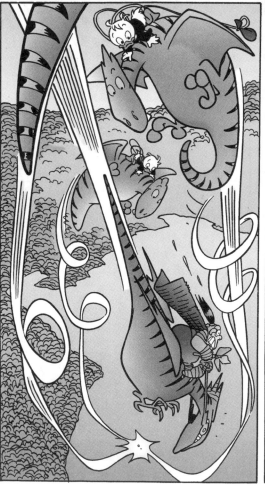

TWANG!!

TWANG!!

!!!

GOOD GOING, GUYS! THANKS!

HEY, YOU *MORG MORON!* STOP SHAKING THE ROPE OR I'LL HAVE TO *DROP* YOU!

BELIEVE ME, IT'S A *LONG* FALL!

÷GRR!÷ THEN KRANG *WILL* FALL...

...BUT SO WILL *DUCK CREATURES!*

YANK!

BACK IN TOOM—

A *SECRET TUNNEL* UNDER THE WALLS? *PERFECT!* IT TIES IN NICELY WITH *MY* PLAN!

WHICH IS*? TALK*, McDUCK! I'VE TOLD YOU THE RESISTANCE PLAN— IT'S TIME FOR YOU TO REVEAL *YOURS!*

OKAY! IT CAME TO ME WHEN I REALIZED WHAT A *HOT-HEAD* GENERAL HYRRR IS! HE CAN BE *GOADED* INTO DOING JUST ABOUT *ANYTHING!*

SUCH AS *EMPTYING* TOOM OF MORG WARRIORS TO STAGE A FOOLISH *HEAD*-ON ATTACK ON THE FREE HUMANS!

YOUR FRIENDS CAN EASILY *EVADE* HYRRR'S ARMY, BUT JUST IN CASE, MY NEPHEW HAS *SABOTAGED* THEIR WEAPONS!

THE *POINT* IS THAT WHILE HYRRR'S ARMY IS *GONE*, IT SHOULD BE *NO PROBLEM* FOR US SLAVES TO *ESCAPE!*

STILL, THE WHOLE PLAN DEPENDS ON GETTING RID OF *LORD MORAQ!* HE'S TOO *SMART* TO LEAVE TOOM *DEFENSELESS!*

WHICH IS WHY I'M GOADING HYRRR INTO *CHALLENGING* LORD MORAQ!

AND WHY I'LL EVEN *HELP* HYRRR *WIN!*

I BID YOU *WELCOME*, FRIENDS! IT IS GOOD TO SEE YOU AGAIN!

OHMIGOSH! THAT'S *BRENDON*! JUTE WILL BE *GREEN* WITH ENVY!

JUTE SENT US A *MESSAGE* VIA CARRIER PIGEON THAT WE SHOULD *EXPECT* YOUR ARRIVAL...

...BUT HE DID *NOT* SAY THAT WE SHOULD EXPECT SUCH A *SPECTACULAR* ENTRANCE!

OR DO YOU *NORMALLY* ANNOUNCE YOURSELVES BY DROPPING A *MORG WARRIOR* FROM THE SKY?

WHAT I WANT TO KNOW IS WHY YOU DROPPED HIM ON *MY* HOUSE?!

ARE YOU STILL *MAD* ABOUT THOSE MORG LIGHTNING BOLTS THAT *GOT BY ME* WHEN WE FIRST MET?

≈ULP!≈ N-N-NO, SIR! *HONEST!* IT WAS AN *ACCIDENT!*

AW... *TOO BAD!* I WAS HOPING YOU DID IT ON *PURPOSE!*

HA HA HA HA HA! NOW *THAT* WOULD HAVE BEEN A GREAT *PRACTICAL JOKE!*

HINTERMANN, OLD FRIEND— DON'T YOU HAVE *BETTER* THINGS TO DO THAN *TEASE* OUR GUESTS?

WELL, YEAH... SOMEONE'S GOT TO *TIE UP* THAT MORG BEFORE HE *COMES TO!*

AND I'VE GOT TO *REALIGN* THESE *MAGIC CRYSTALS!* YOUR MORG SCRAMBLED THEM WHEN HE LANDED!

IF IT'S NOT DONE *PROPERLY,* THE SPELL THAT *DISGUISES* OUR REFUGE FROM BEING SEEN FROM THE AIR WON'T WORK!

I'LL NEVER *FOR-GIVE* YOU FOR THIS, BRENDON! *NEVER!!* IF MAN WAS *MEANT* TO FLY...

D/D 2000-004

D/D 2000-004

...HE'D HAVE BEEN BORN WITH *WINGS!*

I DON'T THINK BRENDON IS *LISTENING,* Mr. HINTERMANN!

HE'S TOO... *ECSTATIC* ABOUT *HIS* FIRST FLIGHT TO PAY ATTENTION TO ANYTHING ELSE!

109

AND IN TOOM—

THOK!

AH! THERE'S NOTHING LIKE *HEWING LOGS* TO TAKE THE EDGE *OFF* A SWORD!

SO! CAUGHT YOU *SABOTAGING* MORG WEAPONS!

JUTE! DOGGONE IT, DO YOU *ALWAYS* HAVE TO *SNEAK UP* ON ME LIKE THAT?!

NO, I DON'T *HAVE TO*, BUT IT SURE IS *FUN!*

WHAT DO YOU *WANT*, ANYWAY?

TO DELIVER *THIS* FROM RASMUS! HE SAID TO TELL YOU TO *PASS IT ON* TO SCROOGE!

IT'S JUST FILLED WITH POWDERED ROOTS AND HERBS, BUT FOR SOME REASON, IT'S *URGENT!*

⸗SIGH!⸗ "OURS IS NOT TO QUESTION WHY..."

ANY NEWS FROM THE *BOYS?*

NOT YET, BUT I'M SURE THEY'RE FINE! *DON'T WORRY* ABOUT IT!

STILL, I SHOULD HAVE HEARD *SOMETHING* FROM BRENDON BY NOW!

113

ELSEWHERE—

IT'S ALL *OUR* FAULT, YOU KNOW! *WE* BROUGHT THAT MORG HERE!

NOW THAT HE'S *ESCAPED*, HE'LL HOTFOOT IT TO TOOM AND TELL LORD MORAQ THE *LOCATION* OF FREEDOM MARSH!

THAT'S PROBABLY WHAT THEY'RE DISCUSSING IN THE *TOWN MEETING* BRENDON CALLED!

Yeah... I BET THEY'LL DECIDE TO *MOVE* THE WHOLE VILLAGE!

WONDER WHAT THEY'LL DECIDE TO DO WITH *US?!*

SLURP!

Oh, *CHEER UP*, YOU BIG BABIES! AT LEAST YOUR *DRAGONS* STILL LOVE YOU!

BESIDES, *BRENDON* WILL FIGURE OUT WHAT TO DO! HE *ALWAYS* DOES!

ISN'T HE *WONDERFUL?!*

SO WE'VE *HEARD* FROM A FRIEND OF OURS...

...IN *TOOM!*

BUT WHO *IS* BRENDON? SOME KIND OF *CHIEFTAIN?*

NO, *SILLY!* HE SAYS HE'S JUST A SIMPLE *FARMER!*

BUT WHEN THE MORG EXPANDED THEIR EMPIRE AND *OVERRAN* HIS FARM, BRENDON *REFUSED* TO SUBMIT!

"HE GATHERED UP THE FEW FREE HUMANS LEFT IN THIS REGION, FORMED A BAND OF *REBELS,* AND STARTED TO *FIGHT BACK!*"

"THE REBELS SEEMED TO STRIKE *EVERYWHERE,* WITH THE RESULT THAT SOON..."

"...NO ORDINARY MORG FELT SAFE OUTSIDE OF TOOM!"

BOM! BOM! BOM!

"THEN WHEN HINTERMANN ARRIVED FROM THE EASTERN KINGDOMS WITH STRANGE MAGICS..."

"...EVEN THE DRAGONLORDS BEGAN TO FEAR!"

THAT'S HOW BRENDON'S HELD THE MORG IN CHECK FOR OVER TEN YEARS!

WOW! NO WONDER LORD MORAQ HATES BRENDON!

THE MORG CAN'T EXPAND THEIR EMPIRE AS LONG AS HE'S IN THE WAY!

Ok, THESE BABIES ARE JUST SOOOO CUTE! CAN I HAVE A RIDE ON ONE OF THEM?

RIGHT AFTER BRENDON FINISHES TELLING YOU THE WONDERFUL PLAN HE'S COME UP WITH!

MORE ALE, MY LORD?

BAH! IT TASTES OF *DIRT!* HAVE THE BREWER *FLOGGED!*

YES, MY *LORD!*

ARMIES OF THE MORG— LORD MORAQ IS A *WEAK FOOL!*

MORAQ CAN *NOT* LEAD THE MORG TO *VICTORY!*

BUT GENERAL HYRRR *CAN!* THAT IS WHY GENERAL HYRRR *CHALLENGES* MORAQ FOR *LORDSHIP* OF *TOOM!*

119

YE CATS! THAT HERBAL *STOMACH ACHE* I PUT IN LORD MORAQ'S ALE BETTER HIT HIM *SOON...*

SOK!
BIF!
POW!

...OR GENERAL HYRRR'S A *GONER*— AND SO ARE MY *ESCAPE PLANS!*

URP! ?

HOOLK!

HOOLK! HOOLK! HOOLK!

HOOLK!...

RRAAR!

Hoolk!

WHAM!

BUT *DADDY!* IT'S NOT *FAIR!*

THE COUNCIL HAS *DECIDED,* SILIA! THE NON-COMBATANT VILLAGERS *WILL* BE *EVACUATED—* INCLUDING *YOU!*

MAMA WILL TAKE *HER* BABIES TO A *SAFE* PLACE, THEN RETURN HERE TO *JOIN* ME...

...IN LEADING THE MORG ARMY INTO THE WORST *AMBUSH* IN ITS LONG, BLOODY HISTORY!

Uh... WHAT ABOUT *US?*

DO WE GO WITH THE *VILLAGERS...*

...OR WITH MAMA AND THE *BABIES?*

NEITHER, BOYS!

I'M SENDING YOU *HOME!*

WORLD OF THE DRAGONLORDS
CHAPTER 9: TOOM RAIDERS

NO?! WHAT DO YOU MEAN BY "NO"? YOU *CAN'T* REFUSE!

HINTERMANN'S *RIGHT*, YOU STUPID BOYS! WHAT BRENDON SAYS *GOES!*

NO! AND THAT'S *FINAL!* WE'RE *NOT* LEAVING THIS WORLD WITHOUT OUR *UNCAS!*

IN FACT, IF THE SITUATION IS AS BAD AS YOU SAY, WE THINK IT'S TIME TO *RAID* TOOM AND *RESCUE* THEM!

WE COULD SWOOP IN AT *NIGHT*, PICK UP OUR UNCAS...

...AND BE *GONE* BEFORE THE MORG EVEN KNEW WE WERE THERE!

≈GAAH!≈ THEY'RE *CRAZY!* STARK RAVING *MAD!*

YOU'RE *DETERMINED* TO DO THIS? *ALL* OF YOU?

ALL OF US!

123

SKREE!

IT APPEARS MAMA IS *ALSO* WITH YOU!

VERY WELL! BUT WE'LL NEED TO GET A MESSAGE TO *JUTE* SO YOUR UNCLES WILL BE *AVAILABLE* FOR RESCUE!

HINTERMANN, WHIP UP SOME KIND OF *MAGICAL DIVERSIONS*, JUST IN CASE SOMETHING GOES *WRONG!*

SILIA, GET *PACKED!* I WANT YOU *EVACUATED* BEFORE WE LEAVE!

"WE"?!

THAT'S RIGHT... HINTERMANN AND I ARE *JOINING* THE RAID!

WE CAN'T LET THE BOYS HAVE *ALL* THE FUN!

SKREEE!

!!!

125

BRENDON? KRANG FOUND BRENDON?!

Y-Y-YES, GENERAL HYRRR! A-A-ALL THE R-R-REBELS!

AT LAST! THE WAITING IS OVER! AT LAST THE MORG CAN ATTACK!

SUMMON THE BATTALION COMMANDERS! LORD HYRRR WILL GIVE MARCHING ORDERS!

Y-Y-YES, LORD HYRRR!

SLAVE SCROOGE WILL REMAIN AND ADVISE LORD HYRRR! WATCH FOR TRAITORS IN THE RANKS!

AS LORD HYRRR COMMANDS, SO SHALL IT BE!

WHY IS KRANG STILL HERE? HYRRR GAVE KRANG DIRECT ORDER!

Uhhh... KRANG IS EXHAUSTED! KRANG HAS RUN FOR HOURS TO BRING LORD HYRRR THE NEWS!

THEN LORD HYRRR WILL HELP KRANG LEAVE!

BACK IN DUCKBURG—

YOU'RE RIGHT, GYRO... WE CAN'T START LOOKING UNTIL WE KNOW *WHERE* TO START, BUT STILL...

ALL RIGHT... YES, YOU TOO... TALK TO YOU LATER!

MAYBE THE *ENTERTAINMENT NEWS* WILL GET MY MIND OFF THEM...

...NEW *CHARACTER ACTOR* HAS CAUSED SUCH A *SENSATION* THAT "GALACTIC DOOM" IS BEING *REWRITTEN* TO GIVE HIM A *BIGGER* ROLE!

CLICK!

GROOB, TELL THE FANS ABOUT YOURSELF!

GROOB DOES NOT KNOW WHAT "FANS" IS! GROOB IS *MORG WARRIOR*, ARRIVED ON STUPID PLANET THROUGH *GLOWING HOLE IN SKY!*

GROOB FOUGHT *TWO* HUMANS AND *FIVE* DUCK CREATURES! GROOB WAS *CHEATED!* GROOB *LOST!*

WHEN GROOB CAME TO, HUMANS AND DUCK CREATURES WERE *GONE*, AND SO WAS HOLE IN SKY! GROOB IS *STRANDED* HERE!

WHERE IS FOOD? GROOB IS HUNGRY!

ISN'T HE *AMAZING?!* HE NEVER *BREAKS CHARACTER!*

FIVE DUCKS?

GYRO! THE TRAIL JUST GOT *VERY HOT!*

ONE MINUTE BEFORE MIDNIGHT—

MIDNIGHT!

WHAM!!

FIRE! FIRE IN THE STABLES!

CLANG! CLANG! CLANG!

COME! FIRE IS ALWAYS GOOD SPORT!

IF FATE IS KIND, PERHAPS SLAVE OR TWO WILL BURN!

UNCA DONALD!!!

MAN, IT'S GOOD TO SEE YOU LITTLE SQUIRTS!

WAIT A MINUTE! *WHERE'S UNCA SCROOGE?*

I... I'M SORRY! I *COULDN'T* GET HIM HERE! HE'S IN THE WAR ROOM WITH LORD HYRRR, MAKING *BATTLE PLANS!*

TOUGH BREAK, BUT *BRENDON!* WE HAVE TO *GO!* THOSE SENTRIES WON'T BE DISTRACTED BY A FIRE FOR LONG!

B-B-B-BRENDON?!!

WE CAN'T JUST *ABANDON* HIM, BRENDON!

PLEASE!

BATTLE PLANS? FOR THE MORG ATTACK ON *US?*

SORRY, OLD FRIEND! WE CAN'T LEAVE TOOM YET!

I WANT TO KNOW WHAT THAT *OLD DUCK* KNOWS!

SORRY, GUYS, BUT WE NEED YOU TO BE *TOO FREAKED* TO FOLLOW!

SKREE!

SKREE!

POW!

POW!

POW!

YAHOO!! WE ALL *MADE IT!*

I JUST HOPE *BRENDON* DOES TOO! HE'S GOT THE *HARD* PART!

BY THE SKULLS CRUSHED IN MORG CONQUESTS! HAS TOOM GONE *MAD?!*

WHOOSH!!!

NO... YOUR *STUPIDITY* MAKES YOU TOO *VALUABLE,* "LORD" HYRRR!

BESIDES, *THIS* IS WHAT I CAME FOR!

RESIST!

≈SCREECH!≈ HELP! MY LORD— *SAVE* ME!

NO! I DON'T WANT TO BE ABDUCTED BY *HAIRLESS MONKEYS!!!*

ARRGH!

~WHEW!~ SO *THAT'S* BRENDON*!* I STILL CAN'T BELIEVE I *MET* HIM*!*

WHAT'S MORE, HE EVEN *TALKED* TO ME! LET ME BE PART OF *HIS* PLAN*!*

I CAN'T WAIT UNTIL HE *LIBERATES* TOOM SO I CAN SEE HIM AGAIN*!* WONDER IF HE'LL *REMEMBER* ME?

GOSH, WOULDN'T IT BE SOMETHING IF HE *DID?* WOULDN'T IT BE SOMETHING IF HE LET ME *JOIN* HIS ARMY*?!*

BOY IS UNDER *ARREST!*

SNIFFLES

SMOKEY

SHREEE!

SPITFIRE

MAMA

WORLD OF THE DRAGONLORDS
CHAPTER 10: FAMILY MATTERS

D/D 2000-006

SORRY, UNCA DONALD, BUT WE'RE GONNA HAVE TO *EAT AND RUN!*

WE'VE GOT *DRAGONS* TO FEED AND EXERCISE, AND WE DON'T LIKE TO KEEP THEM *WAITING!*

!

I'M JUST GOING TO RUN AND *NOT EAT,* NEPHEW!

THUNK!

BRENDON PROMISED TO SHOW ME THE *SOURCE* OF THE *OIL* THAT MORG TRACKED IN!

AAARGH!

WHAT KIND OF A FAMILY *IS* THIS? WE *NEVER* DO ANYTHING *TOGETHER!*

WE'RE SORRY, UNCA DONALD...

...WE KNOW WE'RE NOT A *NORMAL* FAMILY...

...BUT WE *ARE* A FAMILY— WHEN IT *COUNTS!*

THINK ABOUT IT!

THINK ABOUT IT? *BAH!* I'LL JUST REMEMBER ALL THE TIMES...

≈*UNGH!*≈ ≈*UNNNGGH!*≈ I'VE GOT TO GET FREE AND *RESCUE* THE BOYS!

≈*SIGH!*≈ MUCH AS I HATE TO *ADMIT* IT, *I'M* THE HEAD OF OUR FAMILY, AND I'M *ALREADY* DOING SOMETHING!

YES, THE BOYS ARE ALL RIGHT, EXCEPT THAT FOR SOME REASON, THEY'RE AWFULLY *WORRIED* ABOUT *YOU TWO!*

UNCA DONALD!!!

PLEASE, BRENDON! WE CAN'T JUST *ABANDON* UNCA SCROOGE!

...ALL THE TIMES WE *STUCK TOGETHER* LIKE A *FAMILY!*

139

MEANWHILE, BACK ON EARTH—

ARE YOU GETTING ANYTHING YET, GYRO? FROM WHAT GROOB SAID, THIS *MUST* BE WHERE HE CAME THROUGH A "GLOWING HOLE IN THE SKY"!

FAINTLY... FAINTLY...

...BUT THE READING ON MY ENERGY TRACER IS DEFINITELY GETTING *STRONGER*! I WOULDN'T BE SURPRISED IF WE'RE ALMOST...

THERE!

I'D SAY THE "HOLE" WAS RIGHT OVER THERE! PROBABLY SOME KIND OF *DIMENSIONAL PORTAL*!

CAN... CAN YOU *RE-OPEN* IT?

WELL, FIRST I'D HAVE TO BUILD AN *AMPLIFIER* TO SEE WHAT *KIND* OF ENERGY MADE IT! IT'S GOT A *VERY STRANGE* SIGNATURE!

THEN *BUILD* IT! GYRO, OUR FRIENDS ARE *MISSING*, MAYBE IN *GRAVE DANGER*! WE'VE *GOT* TO *HELP* THEM!

I-I'M NOT SAYING I *CAN'T* OR *WON'T*...

...JUST THAT I SUSPECT THAT PORTAL WAS OPENED BY *MAGIC*, AND MAGIC GIVES ME THE *WILLIES*!

—ELSEWHERE—

HEY, GUYS! LOOK HOW *STRONG* SNIFFLES IS GETTING!

IN FACT, HE'S BE-COMING A REGULAR LITTLE *SHOW-OFF!*

SNIFFLES HAS *YOU* TO THANK FOR THAT, LOUIE!

YEAH, YOU'VE *NURSED* AND *PAMPERED* HIM SIX WAYS TO SUNDAY!

SEEING SNIFFLES SO WELL MAKES IT A LITTLE EASIER TO *LEAVE* HIM!

ACK IN TOOM—

RASMUS! RASMUS! CLARG HAS *NEED* OF RASMUS!

CALM DOWN, MASTER! EVERYTHING IS UNDER CONTROL!

BUT THE ENTIRE GARRISON MARCHES TOMORROW AND CLARG IS IN *BIG TROUBLE!*

LORD HYRRR HAS *REWARDED* CLARG BY PLACING CLARG IN *CHARGE* OF TOOM WHILE THE ARMY IS GONE!

BUT LORD HYRRR IS LEAVING *VERY FEW* MORG BEHIND— ONLY BUTCHERS AND BAKERS AND... AND *TRADESMEN!*

AND THE *SLAVES* ARE SO *DISOBEDIENT!*

JUST LEAVE THE SLAVES TO *ME!* I'LL MAKE SURE THEY DO THE *RIGHT* THING!

AT LEAST THAT BOY *JUTE* WON'T BE CAUSING ANY MORE TROUBLE!

BOY IS LOCKED SAFELY AWAY IN LORD HYRRR'S *WORST* DUNGEON!

YOU *FAT FOOL!* YOU'VE JUST SEALED *YOUR* FATE!

FREEDOM MARSH—

NO NO NO *NO NO!* YOU CAN'T SAY NO TO GOING HOME *AGAIN!*

DOES THIS MEAN WE'RE STAYING FOR THE *WAR?*

DON'T BE MAD, UNCA DONALD! WE JUST *HAVE TO* SEE THIS THROUGH!

MAD? I'M NOT MAD! WE'RE *FAMILY,* RIGHT...

...AND FAMILIES *STICK TOGETHER* WHEN IT COUNTS!

BUT... UH... WHY FIGHT THE MORG *NOW?* WHY NOT JUST *DISAPPEAR* INTO THE FOREST AND SET UP A *NEW CAMP?*

BECAUSE WE'LL NEVER HAVE A *BETTER CHANCE* TO *DEFEAT* THE MORG, THANKS TO HYRRR'S *IDIOTIC* "STRATEGY"!

YOU SEE, DONALD, THE MORG ARE VICIOUS, BUT *FEW* IN NUMBER! THAT'S WHY THEY'RE SO *DEPENDENT* ON THEIR CAPTIVE *DRAGONS!*

BUT LORD MORAQ *DRAINED* THE MORG EMPIRE OF *DRAGONLORDS* FOR THIS *ONE* CAMPAIGN!

IN DOING SO, HE RISKED *MUCH—* THE *LOSS* OF SO *MANY* DRAGONS WILL *CRIPPLE* THE WHOLE EMPIRE!

WE CAN DEAL WITH THE MORG INFANTRY, THANKS TO DONALD'S WEAPONS WORK AND SCROOGE'S OIL IDEA!

BUT FOR THAT IDEA TO WORK, WE HAVE TO MAKE SURE THEY'RE ALL LUMPED TOGETHER IN ONE PLACE!

THAT'S WHY I'VE DECIDED TO ALLOW THEM TO OVERRUN FREEDOM MARSH!

BUT THE REAL KEY TO VICTORY IS THE AIR WAR! THE MORG HAVE 50 DRAGONS, AND WE ONLY HAVE TWO!

NO! THE BABIES WILL NOT BE ALLOWED TO FIGHT!

BUT IF WE CAN KNOCK A FEW MORG OFF THEIR DRAGONS, I'M CONVINCED THAT MAMA CAN RECRUIT THOSE DRAGONS FOR OUR SIDE!

SKREEE!

WAIT A MINUTE! JUST HOW ARE YOU GOING TO DO THAT "KNOCKING"?!

MY MAGIC ALWAYS SPOOKS A FEW! AND WE'VE "LIBERATED" A BUNCH OF LIGHTNING STONE LANCES!

WE CAN USE THE LANCES TO *ZAP* LOW FLYERS, OR MAMA AND I CAN *HARRY THE FLANKS* AND ZAP A FEW MORE!

WE'LL JUST *CHIP AWAY* UNTIL WE EVEN UP THE ODDS!

GOOD PLAN AS FAR AS IT GOES, BUT IT WILL TAKE *TOO LONG!* WE NEED *SOMETHING ELSE* TO HELP US BRING DOWN *MORE* DRAGONLORDS!

BOYS, DID THE WOODCHUCKS EVER TEACH YOU HOW TO MAKE GREAT HONKING *CATAPULTS?*

YES!

BRENDON, IF YOU GIVE US ENOUGH *CARPENTERS...*

...WE CAN SHOW THEM HOW TO MAKE *ANTI-DRAGONLORD WEAPONS...*

...OUT OF *TREES!*

Mr. HINTERMANN, *HOW MANY* LIGHTNING STONE LANCES DO YOU HAVE?

A *FEW DOZEN,* ALL TAKEN FROM FALLEN MORG! WHY?

WELL, I'VE HAD LOTS OF... er... *EXPERIENCE* WITH LIGHTNING STONES! IT'S GIVEN ME AN *IDEA!*

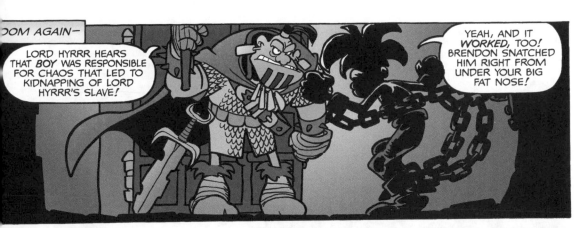

OOM AGAIN—

LORD HYRRR HEARS THAT *BOY* WAS RESPONSIBLE FOR CHAOS THAT LED TO KIDNAPPING OF LORD HYRRR'S SLAVE!

YEAH, AND IT *WORKED*, TOO! BRENDON SNATCHED HIM RIGHT FROM UNDER YOUR BIG FAT NOSE!

BY NOW, BRENDON HAS DROPPED THAT *TRAITOR* DOWN A *VOLCANO!* HE WON'T *FINISH* YOUR PLAN OF ATTACK NOW!

GOOD! THAT IS JUST WHAT *LORD HYRRR* WOULD DO! NOW THE SLAVE WILL NOT *REVEAL* HYRRR'S PLANS...

...OR THAT HYRRR'S PLAN IS *ALREADY* FINISHED! THE MORG MARCH *TOMORROW!*

GASP!

BUT BOY HAS *OTHER* THINGS TO WORRY ABOUT! FOR WHEN LORD HYRRR RETURNS TO TOOM...

...BOY WILL BE THE *MAIN ENTERTAINMENT* IN LORD HYRRR'S *VICTORY CELEBRATION!*

CLING!

147

GENERAL SNARK REPORTING AS ORDER-ED, LORD HYRRR!

GOOD! IS ALL PROCEEDING SMOOTHLY?

AYE! ALL MORG WARRIORS HAVE BEEN ORDERED TO REPORT TO THE *ARMORY!*

"THERE, EACH DRAGON-LORD WILL RECEIVE A NEW *LIGHTNING STONE LANCE!*"

"WHILE THE COMMON WARRIORS WILL ALL BE ISSUED SHARP NEW *BLADES!*"

POK!

WHEN *NEXT* THE RAYS OF THE SUN STRIKE THIS LANCE, LORD HYRRR WILL LEAD THE MORG IN THE *FINAL BATTLE* TO *ANNIHILATE* THE REBELS!

VERY GOOD! BUT DID GENERAL SNARK *BRING* WHAT LORD HYRRR *REQUESTED?!*

AYE! HERE!

BEHOLD, SNARK— THE *EMPEROR'S* VERY OWN LIGHTNING STONE *LANCE!*

WORLD OF THE DRAGONLORDS
CHAPTER 11:
SNIFFLES

XI

WAR.

D/D 2000-007

NORMALLY THE NOISIEST, MOST CACOPHONOUS UNDERTAKING KNOWN TO MAN.

BUT WHEN THIS CLIMACTIC BATTLE IS OVER, THE COMBATANTS WILL SWEAR IT ALL TOOK PLACE IN TOTAL SILENCE...

WITH THE EXCEPTION OF ONE UNFORGETTABLE, HEARTRENDING CRY!

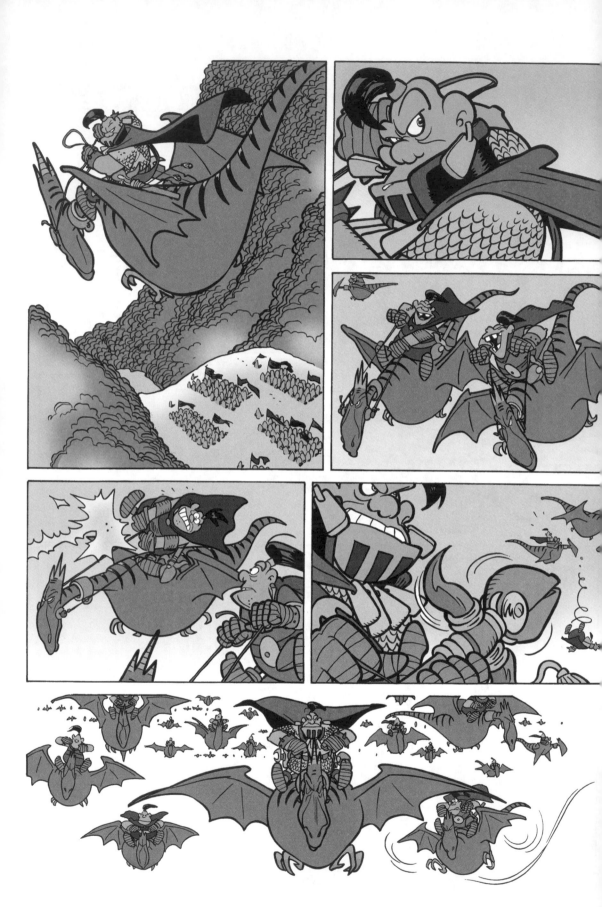

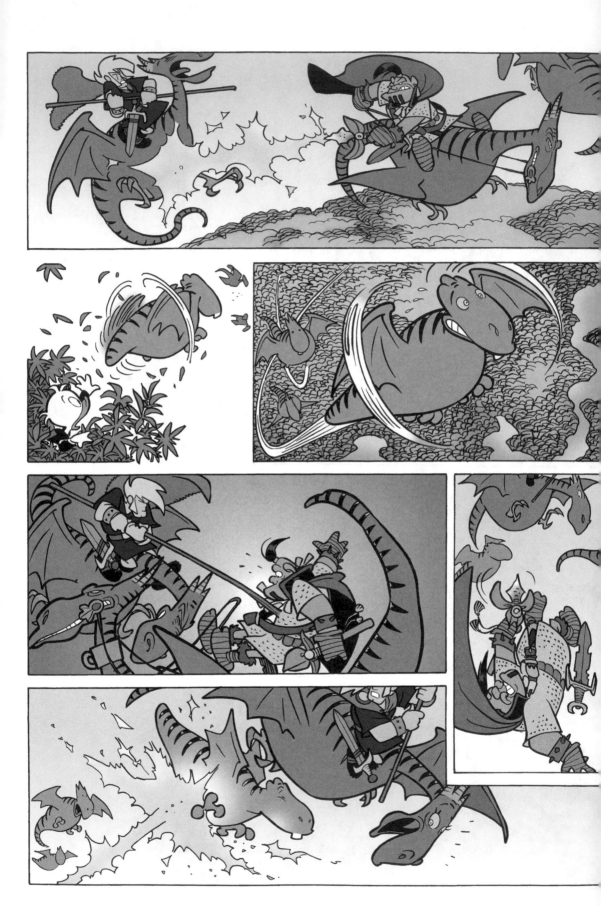

SKREEEE!

WORLD OF THE DRAGONLORDS
CHAPTER 12: HOME

XII

D/D 2000-008

=WAIL! SOB! MOAN!= CLARG DOES NOT WANT TO *DIE* IN THIS DARK DUNGEON!

IF CLARG DOES NOT STOP THAT INCESSANT *WAILING*, HYRRR WILL MAKE SURE CLARG DIES *SOON!*

=WHIMPER!=

A MORG DOES NOT *WHIMPER* WHEN DEFEATED! BETTER INSTEAD TO PLAN *GRUESOME REVENGE* ON THE HUMANS!

CLANGH

=HST!= A *FOOL* APPROACHES! HYRRR'S REVENGE CAN BEGIN *NOW!*

MY MY! YOU CERTAINLY *FILL OUT* THOSE CHAINS BETTER THAN I DID! THEY *SUIT* YOU, TOO!

=SNARL!= BOY *TALKS* TOO MUCH!

BUT BOY WILL *NOT LIVE* TO REGRET IT!

GAK! YANK!

ELSEWHERE—

THE *HUMANS* ARE COMING! THE *HUMANS* ARE COMING!

COWARD!

ZAP!

GH!

FIGHT LIKE *MORG!* MAKE THE HUMANS *REGRET* ATTACKING—

ZAP!

ZAP!

ZAP!

AND SO IT GOES, IN A *LIGHTNING* WAR FROM ONE MORG FORTRESS TO ANOTHER...

ALL THE WAY TO THE *CAPITOL* OF THE MORG EMPIRE ITSELF!

I'D SAY THAT *WHITE FLAG* THE MORG *EMPEROR* IS WAVING...

...MEANS THIS WAR IS *OVER!*

BACK IN TOOM—

I'M *BORED!*

EVER SINCE HUMANS TOOK OVER, TOOM HAS TURNED INTO *DULLSVILLE!* THERE'S *NOTHING* TO DO!

Z!

RASMUS WON'T EVEN LET ME *TEASE* THE MORG PRISONERS ANYMORE!

AND *YOU GUYS* ARE NO FUN! ALL YOU DO IS STAND AROUND AND *WAIT!*

≈SIGH!≈ OH, HOW I WISH *SOMETHING* WOULD *HAPPEN!*

SKREEE!

HEY! HINTERMANN'S BROUGHT *SILIA!*

IF BRENDON SENT FOR HIS *DAUGHTER,* IT'S GOT TO MEAN HE'LL BE *BACK* SOON!

RIGHT AS USUAL! YOU BOYS WOULD MAKE GREAT *SPIES!*

HELLO!

!!

170

YOU MUST BE *JUTE!* MY FATHER TOLD ME HOW YOU *HELPED HIM* RAID TOOM!

AW, IT WAS NOTHING...

!

I'LL SAY! A REALLY *CLEVER* BOY WOULDN'T HAVE LET HIMSELF GET *CAPTURED* BY THE MORG!

HOLD ON THERE, SON! I KNOW SHE'S A REAL *PAIN,* BUT THERE'S SOMETHING ABOUT *BOTH* OF YOU I NEED TO *CHECK!*

SKREEE!

SKREEE!

HELLO, MAMA...

SKREEE!

YES, IT'S GOOD TO BE *BACK!*

SOMEWHAT LATER—

JUTE, MAY WE HAVE A WORD WITH YOU?

Um... HINTERMANN HAS DONE SOME *TESTS* ON YOU AND SILIA, AND, Uh...

Oh, SAY IT STRAIGHT OUT! THEY'RE *BROTHER AND SISTER!*

WHAT?! NO *WAY!* I CAN'T BE RELATED TO THAT... THAT... *BRAT!* THE GOOFY MAGICIAN IS *WRONG!*

NOPE! NO DOUBT ABOUT IT! YOU EVEN *LOOK* ALIKE!

WE DO NOT!

SO... uh... I TALKED IT OVER WITH SILIA! SINCE I ADOPTED *HER*, IT SEEMS ONLY FAIR THAT I *ADOPT* HER *BROTHER*, TOO!

FAIR? *HAH!*

TH-THEN *YOU'D* BE MY *FATHER?* I... I'D HAVE *BRENDON* FOR A FATHER?!

SIS!!

173

174

WE'RE GETTING *CLOSER!* THIS TIME I MANAGED TO OPEN A *TWO-INCH* HOLE!

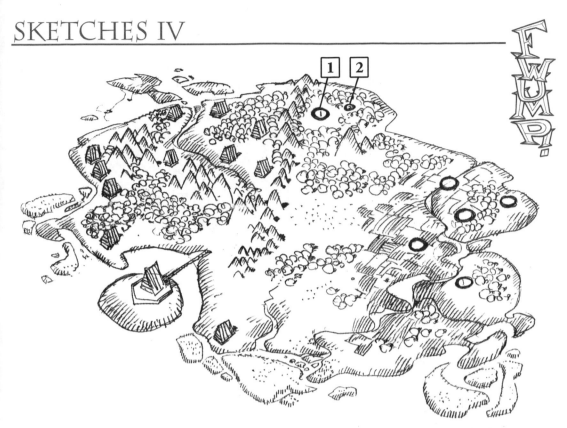

A map of the alternate world. The action in the serial takes place on the border between the Morg and human land, near the fortress city of Toom (#1) and Freedom Marsh (#2).

A design for a street scene in Toom, the Morg fortress.

A rough overhead design of Toom, the Morg fortress city.

A design for the human camp in the forest.

A design for the lightning stone club (discharging a bolt of electricity).

FWUMP!

Model studies of free humans.

Model studies of slave humans.

A design for the dragon stables.

A design for the dragon symbol / logo.

BYRON ERICKSON

Born in Tucson, Arizona on February 3, 1951, Byron Erickson grew up reading far too many comic books, the best of which were the great American Disney comics of the 1950s. "It may be heresy to say so today," he comments, "but my favorite feature in *Walt Disney's Comics and Stories* was the continued Mickey Mouse adventures by Carl Fallberg and Paul Murry, not the classic Carl Barks Donald Duck 10-pagers."

After collecting more than 30,000 comic books, Erickson decided it was time to actually earn some money from that wasted youth. He accepted a job with Another Rainbow Publishing in 1983 to work on *The Carl Barks Library*, a compendium of all of Barks' Disney comics.

Another Rainbow was a small company founded and staffed by fans, and as it grew, Erickson's opportunities grew. As he puts it, "When Another Rainbow got a photostat camera, publisher Bruce Hamilton asked if anyone on the staff wanted to learn to run it. I said I would. Then a complex type-setting machine came along; I said I would learn that, too. Ditto negotiations and relations with printers and distributors. Finally, Another Rainbow got a license to publish the Disney comics in the United States under the Gladstone imprint, and when Bruce asked who wanted to be the editor, my hand went up."

Over the next three years, Erickson discovered and encouraged Don Rosa and William Van Horn, the first work of whom appeared in Gladstone comics.

Erickson also printed high-quality Danish and Dutch productions for the first time in the US.

In 1990, Disney revoked Gladstone's Disney comics license, leading to Erickson's departure from Gladstone. Disney's intent was to publish its own American comic books in-house. The Disney project ended, but by that time Erickson had moved on to Chicago. There he worked at First Publishing as one of the editors of a diverse line of comics that included superheroes, action-adventure, manga, a new *Classics Illustrated* series, Eric Shanower's Oz graphic novels, and *Betty Boop's Big Break*.

Still, Erickson missed the Disney characters. So when Don Rosa prompted Nancy Dejgaard, the Editor-in-Chief of Gutenberghus Publishing Service (now called Egmont Creative) to offer Erickson a job in early 1991, Erickson accepted and moved to Denmark. He has worked at Egmont ever since: first as Managing Editor, then Editor-in-Chief, and now as Creative Director.

Today Erickson still works at Egmont, but is determined to try to write more—at least one story per month. He reports that he is failing miserably at meeting that quota, but is having loads of fun trying.

GIORGIO CAVAZZANO

by Frank Stajano, Ph.D.

Unquestionably the most innovative and dynamic of all the Italian Disney artists, Giorgio Cavazzano began his precocious Disney career as an adolescent. Although Cavazzano has written a few scripts himself, he is above all an outstanding graphic artist.

Born in Venice in 1947, Cavazzano was only 12 years old when he began inking the pencil art of his cartoonist cousin, Luciano Capitanio. Cavazzano's first Disney ink work came when he began several years' apprenticeship under the great Romano Scarpa. In time, he asked his master to let him have a go at the pencils. The first story Cavazzano both penciled and inked was "Paperino e il singhiozzo a martello" ("Donald Duck and the Sledgehammer Hiccups," *Topolino* 611, 1967), scripted by Osvaldo Pavese. Cavazzano's creative curiosity got him interested early on in such great non-Disney artists as Albert Uderzo *(Asterix),* André Franquin *(Spirou, Gomer Goof),* and Benito Jacovitti *(Cocco Bill)*—all at the time unknown to his colleagues at Disney licensee Mondadori.

The 1970s saw the innovative Cavazzano experimenting with a vibrant new graphic style, in which the rubbery quality of traditional Disney characters merged with realistic rendering of machinery and hi-tech gadgets. Cavazzano's best stories from this "techno" phase, mostly written by the gifted Giorgio Pezzin, stood out so obviously from the rest that even very occasional readers recognized and appreciated his work at once. *Topolino* readers of the time fondly remember the submarine of "Paperoga e il peso della Gloria" ("Fethry Duck and the Weight of Glory," *TL* 1007, 1975) and the warplane of "Paperino e l'eroico smemorato" ("Donald Duck and the Forgetful Hero," *TL* 1059, 1976). Cavazzano's subject matter alone shows that he had ventured far from Disney tradition; anyone of lesser talent might have strayed off course in so doing. But, as noted by comics scholar Tiziano Sclavi, "Over the years, Giorgio managed to be Cavazzano and Disney at once. Before him, this had only been achieved by people like Carl Barks."

Cavazzano's influence on other Disney artists has been enormous. Taken as an ideal of perfection by many—if not most—modern Italian Disney artists, Cavazzano was also inspirational to the evolution of his great contemporary Massimo De Vita.

Over the course of his career, Cavazzanno has created an amazing array of comics characters outside the Disney universe, among them *Walkie & Talkie* (1974), *Oscar e Tango* (1974), *Altai & Jonson* (1975), *Smalto & Jonny* (1976), *Slim Norton* (1977), *I due colonnelli* (1977), *Silas Finn* (1979), *Capitan Rogers* (1981), *Big Bazoom* (1983), *Timothée Titan* (1987), and *Jungle Bungle* (1991), not to mention his work in advertising.

Cavazzano has also been the recipient of many comics awards.

Frank Stajano, Ph.D., has coauthored Disney comics reference books on Don Rosa and Floyd Gottfredson. The greatest joy of his life was to spend a weekend at Carl Barks' home in Grants Pass, Oregon in 1998. Visit Frank's web page at http://www.cl.cam.ac.uk/~fms27/. Biography © Frank Stajano used with permission.

© 2005 Disney
Enterprises Inc.

Delivered right to your door!

We know how much you enjoy visiting your local comic shop, but wouldn't it be nice to have your favorite Disney comics delivered to you? Subscribe today and we'll send the latest issues of your favorite comics directly to your doorstep. And if you would still prefer to browse through the latest in comic art but aren't sure where to go, check out the Comic Shop Locator Service at www.diamondcomics.com/csls or call 1-888-COMIC-BOOK.

MAIL THIS COUPON TO:

Gemstone Publishing • P.O. Box 469 • West Plains, Missouri 65775

☐ *Walt Disney's Comics & Stories:* $83.40 for 12 issues, 64 pages ($90.00 Canada, payable in US funds) ....$ _____
☐ *Walt Disney's Donald Duck & Friends:* $35.40 for 12 issues, 32 pages ($40.00 Canada, payable in US funds) ....$ _____
☐ *Walt Disney's Uncle Scrooge:* $83.40 for 12 issues, 64 pages ($90.00 Canada, payable in US funds) ....$ _____
☐ *Walt Disney's Mickey Mouse & Friends:* $35.40 for 12 issues, 32 pages ($40.00 Canada, payable in US funds) ....$ _____
☐ *Donald Duck Adventures:* $95.40 for 12 bimonthly issues, 128 pages ($105.00 Canada, payable in US funds) ....$ _____
☐ *Mickey Mouse Adventures:* $95.40 for 12 bimonthly issues, 128 pages ($105.00 Canada, payable in US funds) ....$ _____

SUBTOTAL: $ _____
SALES TAX (MO residents add 6.975% sales tax; MD residents add 5% sales tax): $ _____
TOTAL: $ _____

Name: _____

Address: _____

_____

City: _____ State: _____ Zip: _____

Email: _____

CREDIT CARD:
☐ Visa
☐ MasterCard
☐ Other

Card #: _____

Exp. Date: _____